THE FLIGHT OF THE BUDGERIGAR

Greetings
from
JGleeson
K9!

THE FLIGHT OF THE BUDGERIGAR

THE AUTOBIOGRAPHY OF JOHN LEESON

The Flight of the Budgerigar
John Leeson
Suite 285 Andover House, George Yard, Andover,
Hants, SP10 1PB

ISBN 978-1-907959-31-8

Copyright © John Leeson 2011

The right of John Leeson to be identified as the author of this work has been asserted by him in accordance with the Copyright, Designs and Patents Act 1988.

All rights reserved. No part of this publication may be reproduced, stored in or introduced into a retrieval system, or transmitted, in any form, or by any means (electronic, mechanical, photocopying, recording or otherwise) without the prior written permission of the publisher. Any person who does any unauthorised act in relation to this publication may be liable to criminal prosecution and civil claims for damages.

A CIP catalogue record for this book is available from the British Library.

Cover design by Robert Hammond
Proof read by Lesley Jones
With thanks to Jack Dexter

All photos from the author's personal collection

Printed and bound by Printech Europe Ltd

This book is sold subject to the condition that it shall not, by way of trade or otherwise, be lent, re-sold, hired out, or otherwise circulated without the publisher's prior consent in any form of binding or cover other than that in which it is published and without a similar condition including this condition being imposed on the subsequent purchaser.

www.hirstpublishing.com

For Judy and Guy

Introduction

'Vanity of vanities, all is vanity'
Ecclesiastes I. 1

It is not the first time that friends have suggested to me that I write an autobiography, and a further prompt from a publisher has probably tipped my vanity scale sufficiently for me not to dismiss the idea completely out of hand. A pebble having been dropped into my pool, ripples seem to have been created, and what follows would appear to be the result.

It is useless to pretend, however, that I have been dragged kicking and screaming into the task of writing about myself, but you must understand that a kind of tension has been set up in the face of my self-imposed assignment. Part of me argues, like Sherlock Holmes to his amanuensis Dr. Watson, that 'the world is not yet ready to hear the extraordinary facts of my case'. Besides that, caveat scriptor! In setting things down in print any writer necessarily reveals more of himself or herself than may originally be intended. Do I really want to be found out?

Thinking about it, my own life is probably no more interesting than anyone else's, and maybe the act of writing what follows reflects as much my pressing need to explain myself to myself as anything else, but I hope I can muster a few significantly entertaining details along the way to prevent this book appearing as mere self-indulgence. Discursive though I am by nature I trust my grasshopper mentality will not annoy.

Someone once asked me to describe myself in a single word, and the only one that rings abundantly true for me is 'complicated'. While this could apply to almost everybody to a greater or a lesser degree I know it to be particularly applicable in my own case, partly because I have been complicit with my own besetting internal complexities for nearly seventy years, and partly because either professionally or otherwise I inhabit three worlds. I even admit to owning two names. Two of my 'lives' are in my own family name John Ducker, one finding me as a wine teacher and the other as a magistrate, and the third is in my stage name 'John Leeson', adopted when I left drama school. Why 'Leeson'? To this day I am not entirely sure although I had a Godmother of that name who was particularly kindly to me, so I suppose her name may have suggested itself to me at the time I was thinking of adopting a separate stage identity. No matter in whichever of my self-professed manifestations I find myself at any one time my aim has been to maintain a kind of 'three-part harmony' within myself depending on which world I am addressing.

Against outward appearances, perhaps, I am a fairly private person with a natural reticence for personal revelations, and you may possibly think it a little perverse that an actor should seek to shun the proverbial spotlight.

Perhaps it is not so surprising after all. There is a sense in which all performers are vulnerable: some wear their hearts more overtly on their sleeve while others opt to hide behind the characters they play. There is plenty of room in the world both for extroverts as for introverts and as an actor I have met many in both camps.

Taking courage from the fact that I have publicly exhibited a fair chunk of my acting career in my one-man show 'A Dog's Life' I move further forward – and the result is what you will see.

Chapter 1

'In my beginning is my end'
East Coker, T.S.Eliot.

Towards the end of March 1943 a celebratory peal of bells was rung to announce my arrival in the world a few days earlier. The gentle tintinnabulation was sounded on hand-bells in the vicarage where I grew up rather than from the neighbouring tower of St Margaret's church, Leicester, where my father was the vicar. Church bells sounding openly in wartime would have been the signal either of dire national alarm or a means of sounding victory, although in this case the victory was a private domestic one: my parents now had a son.

My sister Alison had ten years age advantage over me, my mother having mis-carried another child in the interim between my sister's birth and my own, and my brother Peter was to follow some three years later. I was the proverbial 'middle child'. Thereby hangs a tale!

I suppose every child naturally seeks confirmation of its parentage and identity somewhere along the line.

It is all part of one's sense of 'belonging'. I gathered that my father's family may have hailed originally from the north of England - the name Ducker appears most frequently in the Manchester area - but given his middle name Neilson there was also a suggestion of my father's linkage to a cadet branch of the Mackay clan of Scotland.

Clearly, were I interested, I would have undertaken further genealogical researches but I am not sure that they would be of interest here. Equally the name Ducker may have been a corruption of 'Deutscher' or 'Dutch-er'. One takes one's pick.

My mother's side of the family had perhaps a deeper history: there were some established linkages between her own family name, Payne, and the Chassereau family - French Huguenots – and I have not yet taken the trouble to follow up a secondary suggested linkage to the Despencers: a family whose connections extended as far back at least as Warwick the Kingmaker.

Enough said.

Possibly a rather dismal patch in the undergrowth of English history in any case!

No matter my somewhat foggy lineage, for all the shining potential of a new baby I proved rather a trial to my poor parents: I developed a life-threatening meningitis at the age of eleven months, and had additionally to undergo a mastoid operation. Needless to say I have no memory whatsoever of this early crisis in my life although I remember that my mother showed me a photograph she had taken of me in hospital at the time, sitting up in a cot, my head swathed in bandages.

The fact that I had survived meningitis at such a tender age was considered by all concerned as a miracle, and as a result baby John's status in the eyes of his parents became more than precious. A survivor, no less.

In my earliest days in Leicester, light industry used to proliferate – boots and shoes, knitware, and printing presses. Almost exclusively throughout their pages the 19th century parish marriage records of St Margaret's show the shorthand of 'FWK' (framework knitter) as indicator of the husband or wife's occupation at the time – a prominent knitwear factory being all-too visible beyond the far end of the vicarage garden.

While the parish had been home to many families before the bombing raids of the Second World War, at the time of my early childhood the resident population of the parish had dwindled to a handful of souls. The majority of my father's congregation travelled to church from their homes beyond the parish boundary, generally from the housing estates of the city suburbs.

Wartime Leicester's light industry was less crucial to the war effort than that of Coventry, however the city had still been a significant target for Luftwaffe bombs. St Margaret's church and the vicarage standing alongside it across a graveyard remained proudly unscathed whereas much of the surrounding territory had been explosively rearranged in various places.

Older children, I remember, found the local bombsites wonderful playgrounds and seemed heedless of any dangers they may still have held. Recalling all this, my mind is giving me flashes of the TV series 'Danger UXB' and, especially, the opening of that wonderful Ealing comedy 'Passport to Pimlico'.

My father told me that some time before the war he had been considered as a candidate to have joined the clergy staff at Coventry Cathedral. A truly lucky escape as it turned out as, the history of Hitler's 'blitzkrieg' being what it was, I might not have been here to write what you read.

As you will already have guessed, my upbringing was carefully enfolded within the arms of the Church of England: not only did I have a clergyman for a father but both my paternal and maternal grandfathers were prominent churchmen.

My uncle was sometime Rector of Henley on Thames and by virtue of the fact that my father was also Chaplain to the Bishop of Leicester at the time of my childhood, I had an Episcopal Godfather to boot. It will come as no surprise, perhaps, that I have played a number of vicars myself across my career as an actor.

My childhood home life was shared not only by my parents, my sister Alison and eventually a brother, Peter, but by a girl called Lisa, the daughter of a refugee couple who had made a timely escape from Nazi-annexed Austria in 1938.

Growing up together Alison and the extrovert Lisa were thick as thieves, and I recall they took frequent opportunities to exclude me from the mischief they constructed for themselves in their own girlish private world.

They would often shut themselves away together telling me they were discussing 'serious matters'. How serious these matters actually were had to be measured by the shrieks of laughter emanating from behind their firmly shut door.

One of the peculiarities of our vast rambling vicarage which dated (I guess) from pre-Georgian times prior to its subsequent additions, was that it was haunted. At some stage before I arrived in the world the house had been divided into two, half of it being occupied by the family of the Verger, Ernest Morris. Ernest was surprisingly versatile: he was an archivist, a member of the Royal Geographical Society and a distinguished name in the world of campanology – that's bell-ringing to you and me. His other church duties aside, Ernest was in charge of St Margaret's fine ring of thirteen bells and both he and his family lived on one side of our huge divided house and we on the other.

An old vicarage next to a graveyard, and the presence of young children in the building? It sounds like fertile ground for a ghost story by Henry James or his namesake M.R. James.

Insofar as my own family was concerned, instances of alleged paranormal appearances had been recorded by both sets of grandparents when they themselves were living in the undivided house back in the 1920s and 30s or thereabouts, together with an amount of poltergeist activity.

My mother reported that her own parents had been awoken from sleep by a tall cloaked figure who seemingly pressed them downwards into the bed. This figure had allegedly been seen in the neighbourhood of the vicarage by others.

Sometimes objects in the house itself would appear to 'jump' off shelves and crash to the floor. Just-used small items like silverware, teapots or cutlery would mysteriously and suddenly disappear from view, perhaps to be rediscovered months later in a tarnished state at the very top of the garden – or perhaps to vanish without trace.

In my late teens or early twenties at the time my mother had been called away to nurse my grandmother in her terminal illness I clearly recall that my father and I were alone in the house. One night, around dawn, I was awoken by a scuffling sound which my sleepy state interpreted as either mice running around the wainscoting or my father getting up early in my parents' bedroom next to mine. Having padded round to see him, I learned that he had assumed the noise was from my own bedroom, and that it was I that had created the disturbance.

We both heard the noises again, and pinpointed them coming from the lower landing where unaccountably the light was on. As I investigated, the whispering and scuffling sounds ceased, but I noticed that the light was also on in my mother's sewing-room adjacent to the landing - a further mystery, as she had been away for some time. Curious, I entered the room and felt the light bulb experimentally. It was hot, yes, but also getting hotter, indicating that it could not long have been switched on. I reported back to my father. His expression spoke volumes.

Coincidentally that very day (a Sunday) the house received an unexpected visitor from the past: a man appeared at our front door to announce that he had been a member of the local ARP fire-watch team during the war. My father, who received him, told me that his visitor had felt compelled to return to the vicarage that day to ask if there had been any unusual paranormal activity there since his wartime watching from the church tower.

I don't know what my father's response to him may have been at the time, but he was sage enough to remind me that 'it takes a person to see a ghost' — indicating what is now a very modern assumption: so-called paranormal activity is as a result of our minds playing elaborate tricks on us.

Does this apply to dogs too, I wonder? Our family dog, a golden retriever, frequently used to 'see' something invisible to ourselves within a room. His hackles would suddenly rise alarmingly and, barking furiously, he would chase his quarry around the house, finally cornering it in some room or other until either it had either disappeared from his view or he had barked himself to the point of exhaustion.

Many years later I innocently recounted my experience of these strange phenomena to Lalla Ward (Dr Who's 'Romana No. 2) and her husband at a lunch to which they had kindly invited me at their home in Oxford. The response I received was polite but firmly sceptical.

I had been blithely unaware of the reputation of one of my distinguished hearers at the time, but on the next occasion I get the good fortune to share a lunch or dinner table with rationalist Professor Richard Dawkins, author of 'The God Delusion' I'll learn to keep my counsel on such matters! I can only affirm that I know what I know.

My attachment to my father was always close. Not only was he blessed with a twinkling humour, but he was also the soul of patience in the face of my childhood waywardness. Perhaps it was because he had an objective sense of the early emotional difficulties he could see I was facing.

With his enlightened Bishop's blessing both he and a fellow priest of his acquaintance embarked on training together in analytical psychotherapy. For many years my father ran a dedicated clinic from the vicarage, a uniquely specialised arm of his general pastoral care.

As his son I could obviously not have been his patient; nonetheless he was well connected to other sources of professional help for me across much of the period of my storm-tossed adolescence.

My father's passing in 1976 was not without note. Some years earlier my parents had retired from Leicester to live in a somewhat genteel neighbourhood in Cheltenham, where the cancer that had been diagnosed late because he didn't want to be a bother to his doctor finally caught up with him. I was living in London at the time and at about teatime one day I received a phone call from my mother summoning me to Cheltenham hospital where my father lay dying. Not being a driver myself at the time, I headed immediately for Victoria Coach Station and rumbled my way along the A40, arriving at the bus station at the other end to find my mother already waiting for me there. Sadly I had arrived too late. I learned that my father had died very shortly after six o'clock. My mother and I went to the hospital to deal with a number of formalities and then I returned with her to my parents' house, where I stayed overnight. On retiring to bed later that night I remember my astonishment when looking at my watch: I saw it had stopped at three minutes past six – exactly at the time my father had passed away.

Chapter 2

'and then the whining schoolboy, with his satchel and shining morning face, creeping like snail unwillingly to school'
'As You Like It'

Come to think of it, my very earliest experience of acting took place while I was at kindergarten. Miss Lloyd's school in Stoneygate, Leicester had devised a little play in which I had been cast as 'John Duffer' – virtually the village idiot. I cannot recall what the play was about, and I am not sure if I was typecast into the role, but I do remember it was fun, a chance to show off to an audience of adoring parents. The only detail I remember clearly was that I wore a red spotted handkerchief around my head. I also recall one of the little girls in the play became so excited that she accidentally scratched me in the face ... at least I think it was an accident. I even remember her name: Collette. Where is she now, I wonder?

Performances of another kind were to follow when at the tender age of nine I won a choral scholarship to Winchester Cathedral.

Somehow my parents had contrived to enter me in an audition at Pilgrims School, the choir school – a prospect I faced with not a little nervousness as my sight-reading skills were a bit approximate to say the least.

We all travelled down to Winchester where I spent the early part of the afternoon in a gruelling exam, singing scales, sight-reading, and performing the solo treble part in Mendelssohn's anthem Hear My Prayer - 'O For The Wings of a Dove' which I had learned preparatory to the event.

By teatime the results were through, and the headmaster announced to my anxious parents that I was 'in'. I cannot ever remember seeing such delight on their faces: I was promptly plied with ice-cream as an instant reward.

Although pleased for the happiness of my mother and father in the face of my unexpected success I was inwardly fearful of the future. I would have to leave home for the first time, and a perceived abandonment, aged nine, to a boarding school far away was not something I relished.

At this stage, too, I little realised the pressure to which I would eventually be subjected, as both the daily choir practice in the 'song school' and the time taken as a probationer choirboy singing daily services at the Cathedral would eat substantially into the day, when other school work would usually have to be done. I'd need to make up lost time as best I could.

All too soon I began to fall behind, and the society of an English preparatory school in the 1950s was not without its bullies. A more senior boy was deputed by the headmaster to 'gee me up' and act as my mentor, but he told me he privately preferred to give me beatings in order to keep me up to speed. I'm afraid his penchant for giving me a hard time rather got the better of him. George Orwell's bitter essay on boarding school 'Such, such were the Joys', written in 1947, are a surprisingly stark evocation of my own time at Winchester ... almost point by point.

My letters home quickly announced my sense of isolation, let alone my hatred of the prevailing system. I sent ever more urgent pleas to my parents to rescue me and take me back home...but for them to have done so would have landed me in a kind of double bind. It would be 'my fault'. I knew for certain that by retreating into the safety of home I would have 'failed' my parents' high hopes and expectations of me, and I would then have to come to terms with my own diminishment in their eyes, my own 'disgrace'.

Paradoxically, the enduring legacy of my anguished time at Winchester has been a love of classical choral music.

The Cathedral choir regime was certainly demanding, supervised by the Master of the Music Dr. Alwyn Surplice, a name worthy of a character in a Trollope novel. He may well have been a strict disciplinarian but the sound he was able to coax from a group of prepubescent boys was quite magical. Music-making was my only anchor in my schooling's metaphorical cruel sea. The famous conductor Sir Thomas Beecham's quip 'The English know absolutely nothing about music but they simply adore the noise it makes' certainly applied to me in Winchester if only for a brief couple of terms.

So, 'disgraced', I was eventually taken back into the bosom of my family when an alternative preparatory school was found for me nearer home in Leicester where it was hoped I could survive as a day boy rather than as a boarder.

Such was my emotional fragility at the time that I regularly truanted, spending my days walking the streets and parks but keeping otherwise out of trouble, 'dodging the column' as military parlance has it.

I remember coming up with some elaborate excuses, and I dare say my deceptions were somewhat threadbare – but looking back it is clear how very insecure and dissociated I was at the time. Patchy though my school attendances certainly were, whether through wilful absence or feigned illnesses, there was another hurdle ahead of me, and one I could not ignore. The Common Entrance Exam – the portal to admission to the next stage in my education. Somehow I scraped through, and found myself heading willy-nilly for another boarding school, Bryanston.

As a building, Bryanston House was certainly designed to impress. The very last of the grand stately homes of England, designed by Norman Shaw for the second Lord Portman and occupied by the Portman family for only thirty years, it fell to be sold off as a school in 1928.

The present-day school complex, much enlarged since my own day, nestles in its own valley in 450 acres of rolling Dorset countryside, almost like a French château.

The liberal ethos espoused by the school as a place of learning obviously appealed to my parents: 'self-discipline as a framework for self-development' being the watchword for its pupils. Grey flannel shorts were worn as part of the school uniform even in the sixth form, (even the masters wore them back in the '30s ... my!) and school days began early with a cold bath and a brisk walk before breakfast. *Mens sana in corpore sano* I guess. I usually waited at the back of the queue of bath-plunging naked boys as, by the time I had to douse myself, the water was possibly a degree or so less icy. The first thing I learned as a new boy was that 'a breach of common sense is a breach of school rules', which certainly sounded fair enough.

I well remember my admission interview with the legendary headmaster of the time, Thorold Coade:

'Ah, so you are a clergyman's son. We can expect a lot of trouble from you!'

He little knew at the time how true his half-jesting remark would prove.

Although Bryanston was certainly a congenial place in which to study, even there my earlier dissociative behaviour began to take its toll. I greatly relished English, partly because it included essay-writing which I now realise was an escape-tunnel into the imagination.

I dabbled in music too as a timpanist with the school orchestra and was elected as secretary both of the junior debating society and, yes, the junior dramatic society!

For those such as myself who belonged arguably to 'the aesthetes' rather than 'the hearties' there was an enlightened alternative to playing sport called 'pioneering'. This could take various forms: working on the farm or elsewhere on the Bryanston estate, or even helping to construct buildings. A capacious open-air theatre built of breeze-blocks had been 'pioneered' by preceding generations of boys – and I myself became reasonably proficient as a bricklayer.

But yes, drama was the thing!

My theatrical debut at Bryanston was as Feste in Shakespeare's 'Twelfth Night' – admittedly with an all-male cast. Was this a turning point? Acting in school plays was certainly one of the happiest of disciplines for me, and I dare say that Bryanston was instrumental in initiating my lifetime's career. My 'ignition key' of engagement had been turned on – and my world suddenly had a brand-new dynamic... I felt I could gain acceptance, even approbation, by proxy once in the persona of another character.

Whether my juvenile interpretation of Olivia's fool carried any weight in performance is a matter possibly known only to the shade of Shakespeare himself.

By contrast, the last Bryanston production in which I appeared was T.S.Eliot's rather formalised verse-play 'Murder in the Cathedral'. As Thomas a Becket's fourth tempter I was the embodiment of the archbishop's own torn conscience.

For this production, requiring a substantial chorus of 'Women of Canterbury' the school imported a number of girls from the sister school at Cranbourne Chase. A great diversion, as I remember, for boys such as ourselves.

Bryanston itself did not become co-educational until 1972. Perhaps the fate of my later career choice was finally and irrevocably sealed when the school paid a visit to see a RSC production of Twelfth Night at Stratford-upon-Avon.

A magical production starring Dorothy Tutin as Viola, Geraldine McEwan as Olivia and Patrick Wymark as Sir Toby Belch.

The settings, the Jacobean costumes and the performances were quite spellbinding and I remember wanting desperately to be a part of this gentle enchantment, this theatrically created world.

Perhaps I don't need to dwell too heavily on what must now be a familiar scenario. Do I really need to write about my need to leave liberally enlightened Bryanston ahead of due time?

Even there, apart from the occasional chance to perform, I was fundamentally disengaged academically, falling well behind. By this time my parents were much wiser to my deep-seated condition and sought appropriate therapeutic help for me in London. At one point in my teenage years my father had referred me to Dr Frank Lake in Nottingham where an allegedly 'therapeutic' LSD treatment resulted in two distinctly 'Bad Trips', both of which I counted as entirely counter-productive, doing nothing whatever to resolve my difficulties. (I found I could appreciate the 'hell' paintings of Hieronymous Bosch rather better as a result!)

The swinging sixties were awash with this substance as a recreational drug, but my own experience of it led me never to have any truck with it ever again.

The subsequent exercise of analytical psychotherapy was far gentler albeit time consuming, and certainly not without academic disruption. Once it had been put in place I took a day off from Bryanston every a week, travelling to London and back again, my parents bearing the cost of my journeys plus the regular consultation fee to my 'guru in a pinstripe suit', Dr Eric Howe at The Open Way Clinic near Harley Street. Otherwise, my escapes from school were self-generated and cost free. I revelled in the occasions when I could spend weekends cycling far and wide through the rolling Dorset countryside through villages with quaint names like Sixpenny Handley or Plush, or even ruder ones like the Piddle valley and Shitterton.

For all its liberal and liberating qualities Bryanston remained the metaphorical 'round hole' into which my personal 'square peg' did not fit. Looking back I regard my premature withdrawal from the establishment as something of a tragedy. The school was quite exceptional in my own day and a glance at its modern record is heartening, the current prospectus showing just how excitingly it has developed as a place of co-educational learning.

No matter my own personal circumstances at the time I realise just how much of the Bryanston ethos has rubbed off since on my own general attitudes and behaviour. I still blame myself for what I must have wasted of my intermediate education – but life goes on, does it not?

MARKING TIME

So, Bryanston behind me, here I am at home again in Leicester, marking time before any more crucial step in my life but with the need to 'engage' in something worthwhile to keep me afloat and not sinking into depression. My father, in his former rôle as Church of England hospital chaplain, pulls a string with the Leicester Royal Infirmary, and I am taken on as a lowly hospital porter. This was perhaps quite a far-sighted move on my father's part as my new experience would certainly bring me down to earth and put me squarely face to face with the realities of life and death on a daily basis. My very first well-remembered job was to carry the wrapped body of a three-year-old child, the victim of an accidental drowning in a local canal, to the hospital mortuary. Most of my work was subsequently in the A&E department, 'casualty' as it used to be called, where I also remember a Leicester school friend of mine who had been brought in following a serious motor cycle accident. Sadly, despite all efforts to revive him, he died shortly afterwards in the curtained booth into which I had wheeled his broken body. Cruel irony of ironies, his mother, an auxiliary nurse, was working on a patient in the next booth and was completely oblivious to the tragic situation on her doorstep.

Some months later my temporary career as a hospital porter was brought to an unexpected and premature halt by my trying to lift a manifestly overweight patient in a ward at the far end of the hospital. There are ways and ways of lifting, but alas the excess poundage of the patient resulted in my tearing a muscle in my back. To my acute embarrassment and in full view of my peers I found myself being trolley-wheeled painfully the entire length of the building back to 'casualty'. Clearly my patient-lifting days were summarily suspended. That, after all, was primarily what the job was all about.

Once I had recovered, alternative temporary employment was found for me in a small and somewhat dusty independent bookshop.

I can date my engagement with some accuracy – 1960 - the time 'Lady Chatterley's Lover' first appeared in paperback. Never had the little bookshop been so besieged by potential readers, never had there been so many crates of 'Penguins' jamming the back areas of the shop.

On the first day of publication there were queues in the street outside the shop, and the pressure of customers within the shop itself was so great there was neither the time nor the space to get the books on the shelves, so we sold them 'off the palettes' on which they had arrived.

It was a source of some mild amusement that so many customers were buying the book 'on behalf of someone else'. I dutifully read it on my own behalf to see what all the fuss was about. I'm afraid that at the time I didn't consider it D.H.Lawrence's most engaging work.

In those days, and despite my traumatic early schooling at Winchester, music had become embedded in my soul. I remember I used regularly to attend classical concerts at Leicester's De Montfort Hall. This venue was built originally in 1913 as a temporary structure but was possessed of an acoustic that was reckoned to be the equal of the Berlin Philharmonic Hall, sounds warmly enhanced by its sprung wooden stage. It is still going strong. The regular visitors were the City of Birmingham Symphony and especially the Hallé Orchestra with Sir John Barbirolli. I remember two quite spectacular concerts, each in their own different way: one by the visiting Czech Philharmonic Orchestra and Karel Ancerl which offered both the ultimate in virtuosity and a highly distinctive sound quality especially in the wind instruments, and the other a concert by our own National Youth Orchestra.

Being much of a contemporary with them myself I was thrilled by what I heard these young musicians play, and I decided that if they could be so brilliant then so could I.

I even went so far as having an audition to join them as a timpanist or percussion player, but (fortunately) I didn't make the grade. A well-connected musical friend in London even arranged for me to meet the then timpanist of the London Philharmonic Orchestra, a charming man who advised me in the strongest possible terms not to embark on life as an orchestral player.

'When you're on 'timps' you're the orchestra's second conductor, you are out on your own and everyone is after your job ... your standards have to be sky-high ...and some of these 'modern' scores!'

Wisely, I lowered my sights a bit, but I could still enjoy music making at home with the Leicester Symphony Orchestra, a band of amateurs and semi-professionals who regularly gave concerts.

Playing in their 'kitchen' department I well remember my very first concert with them as a percussionist.

The lady timpanist loaned me her personal pair of old cymbals through which she had tied strips of an old handbag she had cut up as makeshift handles. Midway through Berlioz' 'Roman Carnival' overture the inevitable accident occurred – at a particular cymbal crash one of them broke loose and scythed through the air, narrowly missing the right ear of the principal clarinettist and crashing to the stage below. Thank goodness it missed her. I was mortified with horror and embarrassment, particularly as the audience raised a hearty laugh at my misfortune.

I saved up subsequently and splashed out on a shiny new pair of cymbals that cost a fortune, but at least their handles stayed attached!

Chapter 3

*'Then to the well-trod stage anon
If Jonson's learned sock be on'*
Milton. L'Allegro

In her own youth in the late 1920s my mother had been a keen amateur actress and a member of the Leicester Drama Society, an organization not only well-furnished with local talent but also a vibrant part of Leicester 'society'. Having been somewhat stage-struck at school myself it took no persuasion for me to follow my mother's footsteps and join the ranks of the 'Am-Drams' in Leicester's Dover Street. In its day this amateur theatre had been the jumping-off point of Richard Attenborough among other luminaries of stage and screen, so membership was not to be sniffed at.

I am not sure at this point that I had a burning urge to enter the theatrical profession myself, in fact, apart from the dalliance with music I mention, I was quite unsure of the direction my life should take. Somewhere deep within me, though, a seed had been planted, and at the Little Theatre I let a few green shoots pop their heads above the ground. They began to flourish when I gave my amateur stage debut as the over-protected son of the Harrington family in Peter Shaffer's Five Finger Exercise. I was even well reviewed in the Leicester Mercury. A heady success! Thereafter I remember I agonized about taking up the stage as a full-time career and obviously mentioned my concerns to my amateur colleagues. Although one or two of them sought to dissuade me on the grounds that the stage was a particularly tough and sometimes lonely profession and that one needed to be super-fit, let alone super-optimistic, in order to survive its rigors and disappointments, I paid little heed to them. I can only suppose I was living in a bubble of unrealistic expectations at the time.

My parents took the view that if I was so determined to go forward at this particular moment then my gritty determination to succeed must carry some weight in surviving any future the profession might hold for me. I think, in truth, they were happy that I was fully motivated to do something – no matter what, and mercifully they gave me my head.

As it happened the sister of our family solicitor was a local drama teacher, and this lady, Jean Ironside, was promptly enlisted to groom me for the next, crucial, stage in the process of my becoming a professional actor: a drama school audition. Unlike today, when virtually anyone can be co-opted into a film, television or theatre production because they appear to be the genuine article i.e. 'no acting required', audiences in the early 1960s still seemed to place a value on actors who had had a drama school training, who could deal with the heightened demands of the classical theatre, and who could speak 'RP' – (received pronunciation) as in the Queen's English. There were honourable exceptions to the need for drama school training of course: actors who by sheer force of personality and personal discipline of approach had already carved names for themselves in the profession. The previous generation to my own had often come into the business straight from military service and were still 'winning the war for the Allies' in terms of their appearances in the British war films that proliferated in the 1950s and beyond.

So, things being as they were, an audition was arranged for me at the prestigious Royal Academy of Dramatic Art, and I was duly schooled by Jean Ironside in two audition pieces, one from Shakespeare: lines from Sebastian in Twelfth Night, the play that had set me alight in the first place, and one from a modern play – I chose one of the Dauphin's speeches from Jean Anouilh's The Lark - no longer 'modern', perhaps, in the sense we understand it today. Competition for places at RADA was stiff enough way back at the top of the '60s when there were around 300 applicants for the year's intake of twenty-eight places. Today there is an exponential growth in the competition for places: I am reliably informed that, annually, the Academy now has around 3,300 applicants to whittle down to the same bare twenty-eight!

The auspicious day finally came when I travelled to London with my lines tumbling in my head up to the point when my name was announced, and I made my way shakily onto the stage of the little theatre in the bowels of the Academy to be faced by the then principal John Fernald and selected members of his staff. All I remember at the time was the state of my jellied knees which were knocking with fear.

I stumbled my way through the relevant pieces and there were polite noncommittal 'thank-you's from the stygian blackness of the auditorium – so I headed off numbly to St Pancras station and home, trying to put the ordeal well behind me.

The mind has a convenient way of shutting itself down following one's having embarrassed oneself in public, and thoughts of making it to any drama school, let alone The Royal Academy of Dramatic Art, were firmly shelved until I'd regained a lot more confidence.

What, then, was I best fitted to do?

The problem of 'the rest of my life' remained unresolved. At one time I had even entertained thoughts of following my father's footsteps into the priesthood, but I doubted I had the kind of commitment needed to train for it, let alone to flourish thereafter. Anyway it would have been rather more as a sop to my parents who may have preferred me to engage in a less risky profession than the stage.

I didn't have long to wonder: within a month a letter arrived from RADA telling me that I had been accepted as a student. This was almost unfair! I had tried my best to blank out my painful memory of the audition, and now the issue was 'live' again! My next thought was that the letter had been misdirected and wasn't for me after all. But it was awesomely true!

There is a sense in which a drama school is rather like a driving school. In the latter case instruction on 'the rules of the road', deletion of bad traffic habits and a sharpening of one's awareness can be provided prior to taking the test and going out on the road 'solo' where arguably one re-learns to drive for oneself without an instructor sitting alongside.

Likewise a drama school can do much to help one tame one's personal mannerisms and correct deficiencies in one's speech. Equally it can sharpen one's mental and physical awareness and enhance one's ability to listen.

As theatrical parlance has it: 'Helping one to speak one's lines in sequence and to avoid bumping into the furniture'. The business of learning one's craft as an actor, however, happens out in the real world of public performance rather than in the academic hothouse, because, ultimately, a drama school cannot teach you to act. One particularly cherished English film actor, Wilfred Hyde-White, took a typically cavalier view of his own training:

'Don't talk to me about drama schools', he said. 'I went to RADA and I learned two things: one: I couldn't act; and two: it didn't matter!'

I well remember the sense of awe I felt as a new student. The year's intake had been split into two 'streams' of fourteen for ease of teaching. I was already in the presence of starry fellow-students like Anthony

Hopkins (one term ahead of me), Ronald Pickup, Terry Hands (later a director of the RSC), John Castle, Susan Fleetwood, Georgina Hale, Isla Blair, Gabrielle Drake and Nicola Pagett, and a number of other high-flyers, all of whom seemed already to be the finished article, requiring no drama school training whatsoever. I was also a contemporary of Anthony Ainley who will be remembered well by Doctor Who fans as successor to Roger Delgado as The Master, and also of Jacqueline Pearce, with whom I was to appear many years later in an episode of 'Blakes Seven'.

In stark contrast to my peers I myself felt very much like a journeyman. A budgerigar among soaring eagles. I remember Anthony Hopkins in particular whose blazing star quality was such that even when the stage was filled with other actors he was the only person who commanded your attention...just by virtue of his being there. A drama school can't teach you that!

At the time, RADA's approach to drama teaching was eclectic, utilising lots of different inputs from different schools of acting, from 'method' through to light comedy. Doubtless it remains so today.

I remember the Principal, John Fernald, suggesting, somewhat tongue in cheek, that the only difference between a 'method' actor and a non-'method' actor was that the 'method' actor always gets to the punch-line at least half a beat late! Robin Ray, son of the comedian Ted Ray taught essential techniques on concentration; Vladek Sheybal, the distinguished Polish actor who had worked extensively with film director Andrjez Wajda and who appeared inter alia as the chess master 'Kronsteen' in the James Bond film 'From Russia with Love' was a sensitive and illuminating tutor on Chekhov.

Comedy techniques fell to visiting actors like Brian Wilde – ('Foggy' of 'Last of the Summer Wine' fame), and from the redoubtable Richard Briers. Clifford Turner, whose book 'Voice and Speech in the Theatre' had become a seminal voice-teaching manual headed the voice department. I am led to believe he was one of the professionals other than the redoubtable Lionel Logue who was consulted privately by Buckingham Palace as a remedial voice coach to King George VI.

There were one or two entertaining characters on the Academy's non-academic establishment, too. At the helm of Reception was an ex-chief petty officer and member of the Royal Corps of Commissionaires who was known to all simply as 'Bo'sun'. An old 'salt' with a gruff voice and manner who chided late-arriving students with a relish, and dealt with telephone enquiries with a brash kind of gusto.

I remember standing in reception one day as he was taking a call when the one-sided dialogue he barked out into the telephone went a bit like this:

Bo'sun:

'Royal Acad'my of Dramatic Ar'' … 'Who?' …. 'Speak up, I can't hear ya' …. 'Sorry, who'd you say?' …. 'Say it again' …. 'Dame *Who*?'

It transpired it was Dame Edith Evans at the other end of the line whose own plummy yet perfect diction was obviously giving poor Bo'sun trouble!

A few weeks later she came to the Academy to present prizes and immediately endeared herself to her hearers when she started her speech

'Dear fellow-students'.

By the end of the very first term around 30% of new students were seen to bail out for various reasons. RADA was certainly no gentle 'finishing-school'. Drama school training may have unlocked a self-discovery that was possibly too painful for some; others may have simply been unprepared for the pressure and the hard graft that drama training actually entailed.

Particularly during my second year, there was much work rehearsing productions to be put on at the Academy's Vanbrugh Theatre, and there was an unexpected bonus: the Academy's very first overseas tour, taking both 'Macbeth' and 'As You Like It' on the road thanks to a group of enterprising businessmen in Phoenix, Arizona, no less. These entrepreneurs had somehow decided that they wanted to bring a spot of British culture to their Grand Canyon State. Apparently they had initially invited the National Theatre to bring them a couple of Shakespeare plays on tour. 'The National' had apologised that as a fairly new institution they had been established principally to serve home audiences.

The RSC was then approached likewise, but for tour-scheduling reasons of their own they simply couldn't accommodate the Americans at short notice. So, faute de mieux, The Royal Academy of Dramatic Art became their choice. At least it shared the accolade of the RSC as being 'royal' – so it filled their bill. The Arizona businessmen seemed more than happy: they'd be getting top-rated student actors who would not have to be paid! And so it was that 'Shakespeare on the Desert Inc.' was set up. (I remember that, once there, some of the mail we received from home was addressed to us c/o 'Shakespeare on the Rocks'). Programming was put in place to have both Shakespeare plays performed, first in Tucson and then in Phoenix.

Additionally, once in Arizona, we started rehearsing Webster's Jacobean tragedy 'The White Devil' which we would then take home with us to tour around the UK on our return.

This exercise was possibly as much to engage our time usefully and not have us fraternizing too amorously with the locals – mainly shapely High School girls with braces across their teeth who nailed us all to the wall and insisted we talk to them using our 'cute' English accents.

It is not for me to say how effectively this diversionary ploy of extra rehearsals may have kept us all out of mischief – and I dare say in some cases Anglo-American relations were cemented mutually to the very closest limit, but at least the new play got rehearsed somehow.

Between our hotel in Tucson and our theatre there was a mortuary or 'funeral home'. Two of its staff, like jackdaws, were alert to our daily comings and goings and on one occasion they insisted that a colleague and I come into their parlour to witness (and touch) the wonders of wax-based make-ups on the faces of the cadavers they then held in storage. They were proud to show us their wardrobe department too, when the dear departed could appear before the Almighty dressed in a variety of costumes from 'Ol Colonial' to 'Elvis' ... and way beyond. Had they ever read Evelyn Waugh's 'The Loved One', I wondered.

This somewhat bizarre side-trip aside, we had work to do; and generally our performances were received with wild enthusiasm – even beyond the Shakespeare text!

On our opening night in Tucson, when Ronald Pickup uttered Macbeth's quietly ruminative lines:

'The shard-borne beetle with his drowsy hums

Hath rung night's warning peal.' our Arizona audience suddenly raised the roof!

Wild applause, cheering, whistling, stamping! Stunned, at first we couldn't think why, and then – of course – we realised. The Beatles were making their own debut tour of the US at the time, and any mention of the word 'beetle' had connotations way beyond what the Bard – or any of us - could possibly have anticipated!

Tanned, lionised, sated with Mexican food and memories of dramatic and maybe other more personal conquests, our return home brought us down to earth with a salutary bump: a tour of minor theatrical dates in the north of England.

Whereas Arizona had been an almost unreal experience in glorious hot sunshine, the new 'dates' in northern English February temperatures were a taste of what British theatre touring was all about. Early rising, hard slog, quick 'get-ins' and 'get-outs' …and absolutely no frills whatsoever.

We had our first taste, too, of theatrical 'digs', where bedrooms seemed universally to sport the latest vogue in bedclothes: brushed nylon sheets, usually in variegated lilac stripes. One slid around one's bed during the night and out of it in the morning to be greeted by a cooked breakfast sliding equally in a tepid grease. Some homecoming!

Bearing in mind what I have written of my childhood years at home, on one occasion on this tour I had cause to wonder if I might be particularly sensitive to supernatural phenomena. Being the first to arrive in a newly built theatre where the dressing rooms had been built in two towers, one either side of the stage, I bagged myself a well-lit place in a dressing room on the top floor and had hardly put my things down when I heard the door reopen behind me and close again. Obviously another member of the company had rushed up to stake his own claim to a good mirror and a good space…. but no. There was no one in view, but I had the clear sense that someone was in the room with me. Imagination, of course, but I felt so strongly about this experience that I reported it to the stage doorkeeper. He seemed perfectly sanguine about it.

'I expect that's Fred.' he said.
'So who's Fred?' I asked.

'Fred was the foreman of the builders who finished this place a couple of years ago. He died on-site on the very day this building was topped-out. We often hear him walking around the place, slamming the fire doors.'

I promise not to report this to Lalla Ward's distinguished husband for fear of further rebuke!

The Shakespeare plays aside, I had been cast in two small parts in 'The White Devil': one being a Cardinal who announces the new Pope, and the other a grimy back-street abortionist, 'Dr Julio'.

For the latter role I was equipped with a very good if rather grubby grey wig, and I made myself up to look believably elderly and disreputable in my scenes with Flamineo (played by Terry Hands). I had invited my mother to come up to London to see the production when it opened at the Vanbrugh Theatre. I thought at the time she could never have recognized me underneath all my stage makeup, but she told me afterwards that immediately I came onstage she knew it was me because she recognized facial features she had known in her own grandfather who had died long before I was born!

On graduation from RADA some of my contemporaries, including Anthony Hopkins, went straight to what was then the very new, very shiny National Theatre under the artistic direction of Laurence Olivier. A well-deserved achievement, you might think – but others I knew went to The National simply as 'spear-carriers' rather than playing anything significant throughout the entire period of their contract. I remember a chance meeting in town with a fellow student I had known whom I hadn't seen for years… he was so far under the radar that I thought he must have prematurely left the business.

Under the circumstances I hardly dared ask him what he had been doing.

'National Service', he said.

'Ah…' I said, knowingly. Possibly he may have detected a note of sympathy in my voice.

As far as my making a start in the profession was concerned, both luck and good timing were on my side. I think I can say without boasting excessively that at RADA I had finally 'found my theatrical feet' playing Restoration comedy. At the beginning of my finals year I took on the rôle of Sir Paul Plyant, a loving but cuckolded husband in Congreve's 'The Double Dealer' – a part that required the kind of size and stage projection from which I possibly had hitherto fallen short.

It served also as the engine that drove me through to my 'final' finals production at RADA, the farce 'See How They Run' by Phillip King. Here I was cast (to type, obviously) as the Rev. Lionel Toop opposite Angela Richards as my former-actress wife. The play itself relied on madcap energy and a high degree of precise comic timing, delivering a couple of hours of delicious silliness involving an escaped German prisoner, a number of lookalike vicars, a blissfully pompous bishop and a squiffy 'old maid' parishioner. No matter how deliciously funny the audience found the play, perhaps the greatest lesson I learned was that in playing farce one crosses the line of disbelief at one's peril.

To the characters involved, farce is not funny. Farce is real, farce is earnest, and finds its characters as victims of increasingly unlikely circumstance, bravely coping with ever more convoluted situations which, to an audience, are hilariously comedic in themselves. Out in the wide world of the London theatre at the time there were some well-known practitioners who crossed the line of genuine belief and played farce for laughs: a great mistake in my view as this automatically destroyed a delicate dynamic. For me, farce remains one of the great disciplines of theatre and I take my hat off to any actor who understands how the mechanism works.

But I've digressed, and you'll wonder why.

FRINTON

Michael Ashton, the freelance director at RADA responsible for 'See How They Run', had been given the task of directing a summer season of plays at Frinton on Sea. He invited me to join the company at £6.00 a week! Wonderful! Straight from college into work! I do remember, though, that Frinton was just about as genteel and small 'c' conservative a seaside watering-hole as one could imagine. There wasn't even a pub in sight because in point of fact in 1964 the little town hadn't found such things acceptable. Now there actually is one, I believe. By the same token the prevailing mentality thereabouts suggested a suspicion of actors, whose moral background was obviously not to be trusted. We had the distinct feeling on trying to get 'digs' in the town that we actors were the proverbial rogues and vagabonds of yesteryear. Although we were tolerated for a limited period of a six week summer season I guess the local fellaheen made sure they locked up their valuables ... and their daughters.

The 'theatre' itself was in fact the local Women's Institute Hall which had a small stage at one end of it. Our summer programme consisted of six plays, each of which would open midweek so that any locals or summer visitors had the chance of seeing two plays a week should they wish. The moment one play opened we would be straight into rehearsals for the next one. By the same token, of course, we actors had to be not only speed learners, but we needed to carry two plays in our heads at the same time.

There was then the distinct danger that if we had to speak very similar lines in either of the plays we had memorised then we could easily 'jump' the tramlines and find ourselves back in the wrong play...to the confusion of all parties.

The physical sets and backdrops against which we acted were possibly as flimsy as our tenure of the lines we carried in our heads. Rehearsals took place on the same tiny stage throughout our short season and we necessarily had to work 'new' plays within the confines of the current stage set.

To add to the general difficulties the regular director used to plonk himself in an armchair centre stage and have the cast move around him.

'Don't mind me, dears', he used to say, 'I'm just here to direct the traffic.'

My career as a paid professional actor had well and truly begun. However, my professional stage debut was something of a baptism of fire. As a fresh-faced young actor and possibly the youngest member of the Frinton company I was thrust into playing the oldest character in the season's first play: 'Lord Lister' in William Douglas Home's comedy 'The Chiltern Hundreds'.

Despite the fact that I faced the responsibility of carrying the play, I have a clear memory of myself sitting happily with my script in a sunny cornfield just behind the 'theatre', cramming lines into my head. I remember feeling amazed that I was now actually doing the job I had always wanted to do, with the added bonus of being able to sit outside in the glorious sunshine rather than slaving somewhere in a dingy office. Besides, I was being paid the handsome sum of six pounds a week for the privilege!

The part I was learning had originally been one which the veteran actor A.E.Matthews had made his own. The part had suited 'Mattie's' personality to a 'tee'. Dotty old 'Lord Lister' is a crusty character with a lot to say who lives essentially in his own little world, completely at variance with all the other characters around him. At the first dress rehearsal my RADA training in character make-up came into its own, or so

I thought at the time. I was trying to add at least half a century to my own age. Aiming to achieve this I plastered my face with 'five and nine' – two well known basic greasepaint shades - and I drew age-lines in strategic places.

Having dealt with my face as Lord Lister I then had to deal with my hair which seemed to require plenty of white powder. The first time I sat down somewhat heavily in a chair onstage, the audience fell about in fits of laughter. I simply couldn't think why. They could see in the stage lights – but I couldn't – a suspended cloud of the over-applied powder slowly descending onto my shoulders ... and the actress playing Lady Lister sitting opposite me at the dinner table was having dreadful fits of the giggles! I must have looked as if I was sitting in one of those 'snow-storm' glass bubbles.

During the course of the play, Lord Lister spots a rabbit on the lawn through the French windows, gets his twelve-bore gun, shoots it, and sends his butler to retrieve it.

A local farmer had loaned the theatre a 12-bore shotgun, and the stage manager had provided some blank cartridges to fire – but when I fired the gun at the dress rehearsal the explosion was absolutely deafening, and within the tiny space of the auditorium we feared that either the windows might shatter or, worse, the Frinton audience of genteel pensioners could suffer heart attacks as a result. As it was, our ears were 'singing' for a good while afterwards. The theatre manager wasn't too keen on having to pay for a brand new starting pistol as an alternative, but one was provided just in time for the first night which would be fired offstage after I had taken aim with my unloaded shotgun.

I remember stepping to the French windows, taking aim, and seeing the stage manager – a rather willowy young girl - standing just behind a scenery flat struggling desperately to pull the trigger of this pristine pistol, hardly out of its box, and which obviously had a very stiff trigger mechanism. She was also pulling desperate faces at me to indicate that she was not going to be able to fire it.

All kinds of thoughts raced across my brain: should I simply say 'bang' or, at worst, simply throw the gun out of the French windows in the direction of the rabbit – and tell my butler that I'd killed it with a direct hit. Fortunately by this time the stage manager had spotted a random paper bag lying next to her. She had the remarkable presence of mind to inflate it and then to burst it with a slight 'pop' – and I knew that at least on this occasion this was as close as we were going to get to my firing off a barrel at the bunny. If the audience heard the bang it would have been a miracle! I'd have liked to have bought the girl a drink after the show to thank her for her quick-wittedness... but what did I tell you?

Frinton on Sea in 1964? No pubs!

'Mattie', incidentally, was a bit of a legend in his own lifetime. Apparently when he was filming in Portsmouth on 'Carry on Admiral' he was so enamoured of his costume that he insisted on keeping his admiral's uniform on at all times. He used to walk around the town and the dockyards in the full rig hoping that any sailors he met would salute him....which they invariably did, failing perhaps to notice that he was also wearing his favourite pair of carpet slippers at the time!

On an earlier occasion Mattie was rehearsing a play with the distinctly challenging theatre director Basil Dean, the man who founded ENSA, the organization which provided entertainment for the troops during the second world war. The public seemed to think ENSA stood for 'Every Night Same Act – or Every Night Something Awful' – but the letters actually signified Entertainments National Service Association.

Under ENSA's banner, already-established names from the world of entertainment and theatre were officially signed-up to tour both troops fighting abroad as well as playing audiences on the Home Front, sometimes even on a canteen or factory floor.

However on this occasion Basil Dean was rehearsing his cast in an empty theatre with just a few sticks of furniture and with lines painted on the stage floor to represent the walls and the doors and so forth. Needless to say, the actors had to mime opening and closing the doors where none existed.

Mattie was rehearsing a scene when a disembodied voice called out from far away in the stalls:

'No, no, no ... Mr Matthews you've just missed the door and walked through a wall ... go back and do it again!'

The cast played the end of the scene again and yet again Basil Dean called out to Mattie

'No, no, no, no, this is hopeless; can't you see what you're doing? You keep walking through the wall and not the door, do it again!'

At which point Mattie stopped, went up to the place indicating the door and began to mime taking a piece of paper from his pocket.

He then searched his top pocket, mimed producing a pen, and then mimed writing on the paper. Basil Dean, now even more tetchy than before, called,

'For heaven's sake Mr Matthews, what on earth are you doing now?' Mattie called back from the invisible door,

'I'm posting you my ****** resignation - through this ******* letterbox' ... and left the stage!

Six weeks and five plays later the Frinton season was over and our little company was disbanded. It had been a very enjoyable yet surprisingly swift engagement – partly because of the sheer pressure of the work and partly because of the diverting nature of the other members of the company. Suffering, triumphing... we had all been in it together.

Now I wondered somewhat anxiously what might lie ahead for me. I had suddenly become a fully-fledged 'out of work' actor – remembering always that coping with being out of work was all part of the job. Regardless of the fact that I had nothing to much to show as a CV, I felt it was high time that I started looking for an agent.

Many of my RADA contemporaries already had agents of their own thanks to the 'shop window' of the academy's Vanbrugh Theatre, but somehow I had failed to attract one. Equally, the only place I could live and make progress as an actor in television and films had to be London, however, London had to wait.

It was not too long before another job opportunity presented itself, again thanks to Michael Ashton. He was directing a production of 'Wuthering Heights' at Colchester 'Rep, and invited me to play 'old Joseph' – yet another old man. Was I getting typecast, I wondered, or was I just old before my time?

I'd have to say that I remember very little of the production save that once my bald wig and makeup were off at the end of the show I could slip away from the stage door and any autograph-hungry fans quite unrecognized. My disguise ensured I always caught the last train home with plenty of tim e... the autograph-scribbling 'stars' caught at the stage door usually had to rush!

So where next?

Although there was no discernable work for me as yet in the Big City, Lisa, my sister's childhood friend, was the indirect means to finding me a relatively cheap place in London to live. She knew an actor who was looking for someone to share his flat in Chalk Farm together with two other theatrical friends of his. The flat itself was situated a stone's throw from Hampstead, it was capacious, and it was equipped with a decent piano, two cats, Foxy – a long-haired ginger tom cat – and Lily – more of an elderly flea-ridden Astrakhan rug.

To a greater or lesser extent my new landlord, actor Kenneth Waller, became something of a mentor for me.

Ken was a northerner, a fine pianist and singer whose own work in the theatre majored principally on musicals.

Being well connected to other musical actors and professional musicians Ken introduced me to the BBC Club choir, a body of which he was a member, and somewhere down the line I found myself singing everything from Bach to Gershwin with them under the direction of one of the top London theatre music directors of the day, Anthony Bowles.

Sadly, Ken is no longer with us, but I owe him much for the energy he expended in getting me working for myself to find gainful employment. Best of all, he volunteered to recommend me to his agent, Margaret Hamilton of 'Hamilton & Sydney Ltd.'.

A flat! An agent!

Like Ken Waller's cats, perhaps, I felt I had landed on my feet.

* * *

REGENT'S PARK

One wasn't ashamed to use 'connections' when looking for work, and as Ken Waller had himself appeared in productions by David Conville, he was not slow to promote me to him for casting in his upcoming venture 'As You Like It', for the 1965 summer season at the Open Air Theatre in Regent's Park.

The fact that I could sing and that there were a couple of songs to be performed in the show, earned me the parts both of a Page in the Forest of Arden, and also that of Jacques de Boys, not to be confused with the melancholy Jacques.

This character comes on right at the end of the play and, in a single neat speech ties up all the loose ends that Will Shakespeare left lying about.

The play was directed by Harold Lang, himself a distinguished actor, and the cast included Ann Morrish as Rosalind, Phyllida Law as Celia, with Gary Raymond as Orlando.

In addition to the parts I played above I understudied Edward Atienza as Touchstone. Harold had specially commissioned the distinguished composer Elisabeth Lutyens to write the incidental music for the play including the music for the songs, which entailed my taking trips up to Hampstead where Elisabeth lived and rehearsing with her.

'Don't pay any attention to me, dear' Elisabeth growled, banging out her tunes on her Steinway Grand, 'I can only sing the bass line!'

A propos of absolutely nothing, save that it occurred on the way to the theatre, I recall hurrying down a footpath in Regent's Park one afternoon as I was running slightly late. Two very elderly ladies were approaching me, deep in conversation, and all I heard as I hastily passed them was one saying to the other

'Well, dear ... he sank!'

I love picking up occasional 'overheards', but infuriatingly this one will probably stay with me for life.

The production of 'As You Like It', when it ran, was quite magical, the stage settings and costumes redolent of images from the German mediaeval painter Lucas Cranach the Elder, but the weather was such that we were rained off more times than we played. Sodden audiences were issued with 'rain-check' tickets to return on another day if they felt so inclined, but I dare say that for the production company the summer's venture ran at a considerable loss.

DUNDEE

Looking back I am now fairly astonished that I kept myself so busy so early in my career. Further provincial theatre work was now offered, a repertory season on Tayside in Scotland.

The Frinton theatre had been a Women's Institute hall, and the Dundee Repertory Theatre at that time was a converted church. The wardrobe department was way up somewhere near the belfry, set over the stage – and all the heat from the stage lights ascended naturally to the roof.

I remember that on occasion the wardrobe mistress could be found sitting sewing costumes stark naked - even by choice on colder days!

I remember too that there was a very pretty actress who was angling for the affections of one of the male members of the company. During one evening's performance, simply to tease this chap, she stood stripped naked offstage hoping that this actor – who was onstage at the time - would turn to the wings, see her, and be put utterly off his stride.

Her plot failed spectacularly as I recall: she had completely forgotten that her target was extremely short-sighted, and in looking across to the wings, which he did from time to time, he could see absolutely nothing at all!

My time in Dundee was marked both by wonderfully engaging work, everything from Ibsen to Noël Coward, and a wonderful company feeling, thanks in part to the enlightened theatre director Donald Sartain. So busy were we as a company that, through sheer pressure of rehearsals and playing, time swung by to such an extent that I even missed my own 21st birthday. The situation was understandable to a degree as there was a national postal strike at the time and I never received any birthday cards until well after the event itself.

Equally, and unavoidably, I missed attending my own sister's wedding. The season was in full swing, and there was absolutely no chance of my being replaced. I am not sure in her own mind that the saying 'the show must go on' amounted to a reasonable excuse, nonetheless I hope to this day that I am forgiven for my absence. It was a great regret on my part.

I shared rented accommodation within sight of the river Tay with a couple of my theatre colleagues and I have happy memories of cycling off on Sundays, our only free day, to pine-woods across the river to harvest wild chanterelle mushrooms which I would take back to cook for us all ... wonderful with scrambled eggs, incidentally.

At the end of the Dundee repertory season when a number of us were leaving to pursue our careers elsewhere, I remember the chairman of the theatre governors buttonholing me at the formal leaving party and saying,

'John ... we've much enjoyed your time up here with us in Scotland, and we're so sorry to lose you to London. This acting thing ... is it something you're planning to take up when you're down there?'

In the circumstances there really is no answer to that.

Further repertory work followed once I had left Dundee. In Birmingham I was cast to play Antigonus in the Birmingham Repertory Theatre's production of 'The Winter's Tale', directed by Braham Murray. Antigonus is famously the only Shakespearean character to be chased offstage by a bear.

But forgive me, to my shame I must confess something. One of my mother's great hobbies was portrait photography, and she passed to me equally a love of photography in general which I put subsequently to good use to supplement a slender income – or no income at all. When I was 'resting' as an actor I used occasionally to take head-shots of fellow actors for the 'Spotlight' casting directory, in those days a series of thick heavy tomes crammed with hopeful faces giving casting directors at least some impression of what you looked like.

I learned photography at my mother's knee, so to speak, and I was possessed of a good camera, a complete set of basic darkroom kit and a modest talent at securing an acceptable image of my various clients. Thus it was that at Birmingham Repertory Theatre I took casting pictures of one or two members of the company. So successful were my shots of one of the leading ladies that she asked me if I'd mind taking time out to photograph her impending wedding. A great honour. I didn't like to refuse, although taking wedding photographs would demand an ultra-quick delivery of proof-sheets and, subsequently, finished prints. The days of well-nigh-instant digital photo technology were yet far in the distance.

It was to be a quiet wedding, I was told, and I would be the only photographer there. I duly turned up on the day of the great event and ran a number of films through the camera, rushing off to my makeshift darkroom almost immediately to develop them and to print off some proof-sheets.

It was here that disaster struck – the worst disaster that I could ever have conceived. In complete darkness I carefully loaded my tallest developing tank with all the films, but such was my excitement and haste in giving the tank its initial rinse that I mistakenly turned on a hot rather than a cold tap. I realised in horror what I had done almost immediately but I knew in my soul that it was too late. I even went through the developing and fixing process lest there was the remotest chance something could be saved from the wreck I knew I must have created within the sealed tank.

I hardly dared open it for fear of meeting my worst nightmare, but then - there it was – the films had completely melted, and a grey sludgy jelly mocked any pretence I may have held that I was a competent photographer.

A truly awful moment ... with the dreadful weight of an embarrassment ahead in explaining to the bride and groom what had happened.

No, don't book me for weddings!

LONDON

Like many keen young actors at the beginning of their careers I suppose I must have felt tempted to take virtually any acting job for a subsistence wage in order to get a foot on the slippery ladder. For me it was not a matter of wanting to become famous, but simply to get work consistently which would, one day, earn me the respect of my peers.

Today the acting profession has grown exponentially and for 'un-knowns' jobs are possibly even scarcer even though the range of theatre work – street theatre, theatre-in-education etc etc. may have expanded a little. Time is money, and nowadays much casting is done on-line with actors' photos and profiles submitted in a mouse-click, and accessed electronically as a matter of course.

Back in the 60s and 70s, however, writing letters for work was obviously a necessary chore, sometimes amounting to as many as a hundred a week. My two-finger typing skills were put to good use! If I got any replies from the letters I wrote I counted myself lucky, and generally those replies (from casting directors) would say things like 'Thank you for your letter – I already have your details on file' (which had the subtext 'don't bother writing to me again') or 'I am not doing anything at the moment, but rest assured that once I am I shall keep you in mind...' - when one guessed instinctively that the recipient would never remember, and that nothing was going to happen as a result!

Oh, the forests of trees that were cut down in the interests of our writing off for work!

Thanks to the interventions both of Ken Waller and of our shared agent I was cast in David Conville's Christmas production of 'Toad of Toad Hall' adapted from A. A. Milne's 'The Wind in the Willows', at the Comedy Theatre in the West End.

This was perhaps the first of my encounters with animal characters as I was to play Chief Ferret and understudy the incomparable Richard Goolden as 'Mole'. Richard was something of a legend as that character, having played it for fifty years. David Conville, who was also directing the play, made sure that the rest of the company worked around 'Dickie's moves' – i.e. the ones he had learned in the production in which he had been originally cast back in 1930, as apparently they were the only ones he could still remember.

Needless to say, even at his advanced age Dickie was fireproof, despite his having accidentally fallen off stage on one occasion, so my understudy moment for taking over from him as 'Mole' never came to pass. He was the only actor I knew who was capable of having a nap while onstage, sometimes having to be prodded by a 'wild-wooder' crossing the stage from the wings in order to wake him up. But once woken suddenly from slumber he was invariably and amazingly on cue.

THE SMALL SCREEN

At this early point in my career when the television world had not fully emerged into colour I was sent to meet BBC director Gerald Blake who was casting an adaptation of R.H. Mottram's First World War novel

'The Spanish Farm'. The part on offer was that of Lieutenant Mansfield, a young officer in the trenches who had gone 'wire-happy'. More television work was to follow, but my next assignment couldn't have offered a greater contrast: I was cast in a brief storyline as an unlikely guest at Crossroads Motel.

In those days ATV's soap-opera 'Crossroads' represented 'no-frills' bargain-basement daily entertainment and was lovingly spoofed years after its demise by Victoria Wood and her colleagues in her mini-strand 'Acorn Antiques.' Playing heavily on starchy acting and mis-cueing of cameras and performers alike against a background of shaky one-dimensional sets, the comedy spoof was perilously close to the original it sought to parody.

My own brief experience of working on the real 'Crossroads' was bizarre to say the least. For a start I had been cast as a young French hippy, a follower of the works of American transcendental philosopher Henry David Thoreau. Maybe you'll agree that this was an unlikely character to find its way into the storyline of a minimum-voltage teatime TV 'soap'. Rehearsals in Birmingham were skimpy, and I remember that a kind of unspoken hierarchy prevailed both in the rehearsal room and on the set.

At rehearsals no one but Noëlle Gordon, as the proprietor of the Motel and 'star' of the show was allowed to sit in 'her' chair, and there seemed otherwise to be a distinct class divide between the 'regulars' and the 'visitors'.

The detail of the short storyline in which I was involved pales into insignificance alongside my appearance. The make-up and costume departments had kitted me out in a shoulder-length strawberry-blonde nylon wig, a scruffy false beard, and I was dressed in a knee-length toga made of towelling in a shocking tangerine colour. Thank goodness in those days 'Crossroads' was still being recorded in black and white!

I shared a couple of scenes with Collette Gleeson as the character Marie Massinet but the only real drama that befell turned out to be quite unplanned. Midway through the studio recording session one of the studio lights crashed noisily from the gantry far above our heads onto the studio floor, interrupting a scene where two other characters were in deep discussion about whether or not to adopt a baby. It was a miracle that nobody had been standing beneath it. Needless to say the scene was disturbed, the actors looking around wildly in alarm – but the floor manager's frantic waving urged them to continue their scene regardless. They, Collette and I had assumed that the studio would come to halt straight away, but no! The floor manager then cued our own scene which followed on. There appeared to be no time for retakes of any kind, and I assumed that the visual hiatus would be dealt with subsequently in the edit. No such luck. I saw the transmission some two weeks later when the deafening crash, the palpable alarm of the actors and the hesitant continuation of their disturbed scene was broadcast uncut for posterity.

That was 'Crossroads', of blessed memory.

ACROSS A CROWDED ROOM

The address No.1 Fawcett Street, London SW10, a stone's throw from the Fulham Road, has unexpectedly played a key role in my life. I have never lived there, nor to this day do I know who lives there, but it was the address at which a party was held and where, completely accidentally, my future wife and I were to meet. Ironically neither she nor I had been personally invited to it! Neither of us were pure gatecrashers, however. The actress 'nakedly in the wings' at Dundee repertory theatre had me in tow that evening simply as a good friend, nothing more, and Judy had tagged along with a couple of girlfriends, one of whom was celebrating her last night of 'singledom'.... but such was the freewheeling party scene in Kensington in the swinging 1960s that nobody seemed to keep tabs on a guest-list. I dare say the room may have been smoke-filled at the time, and across it ... something clicked between Judy and myself which was more than mere friendship – besides, she confided that she had never met an actor who was actually working, let alone one playing and understudying furry creatures in 'Toad of Toad Hall' at the time.

We agreed to meet again but fate threatened to take the upper hand: Judy was all set to start a contract working for FAO, the Food and Agriculture

Organization of the United Nations, based in Rome. Once the Christmas season of 'Toad' was over I, likewise, was booked for a theatre season away from London again. We vowed to keep in touch, and such was the flow of correspondence between us across our year apart that it eclipsed even my best efforts at scribbling off for work.

Life in Rome certainly seemed to suit Judy, meanwhile I was head-down in productions at Newcastle Playhouse. Her frequent postcards to me were eagerly awaited, and I particularly liked one where she told me she was having a wonderful lunch-break in central Rome, sitting in glorious sunshine in the middle of a huge Pizza. Spelling was perhaps not her forte!

NEWCASTLE

Newcastle Playhouse, the theatre company I had joined, was a satellite of Nottingham Playhouse under the overall artistic direction of John Neville, but were you to drive down Benton Bank in Newcastle today there would be no sign of what was locally known as 'The Flora Robson Theatre'. Having fallen into disuse some years earlier it was demolished in 2009 to make way for road improvements.

My 'digs' were initially in Wallsend on the coast, my landlord being a bus driver whose broad Geordie dialect was all but impenetrable. What surprised me not a little was the fact that he found my own 'southern speech' equally difficult to comprehend. It took us about a fortnight before we became attuned to each other's wavelength, by which time alternative 'digs' had been found for me much nearer the theatre in Jesmond.

One production in particular stands out as the highlight of the Playhouse season: 'The Hostage,' Brendan Behan's rumbustious tragi-comedy, in which I was cast to play the character of Mr Mulleady. Apparently Behan had written the play originally in Gaelic for 'drinking money' of £150, its subsequent English version having been popularised by Joan Littlewood's theatre company but whatever its history there was a call for a great deal of 'the black stuff' to be consumed onstage during the course of the play. The director Bill Hays made absolutely sure that Guinness flowed as liberally onstage as backstage throughout the play, and I admit having only a hazy notion of the final dress rehearsal, let alone of the first night.

Come to think of it maybe Bill didn't either. The Newcastle audience adored the production as much as we did ourselves. It was the hit of the season! When I left to return to London rehearsals for the Newcastle Playhouse season's 'grand finale' were in full swing: 'Close the Coal-House Door', Alan Plater's politically charged musical celebration of Geordie-land.

I had been disappointed not to have been able to muster a passable Geordie accent myself, and I thought it better to bow out of the play rather than display my vocal deficiencies - especially to a Tyneside audience. I had even sought help from Alex Glasgow, the noted Tyneside writer and entertainer who had written the songs for the show. He was a patient tutor, but though I love the Geordie accent, its 'music' is on a different planet from the one I inhabit. It was the parting of the ways.

A SECOND STRING

Through Judy's recently married friend Kate, the original invitee at the party in Kensington, I was introduced to yet another strand of employment to help tide over periods when I was out of work. Her husband David was head of Presentation at the BBC in Manchester, and he suggested I came up at weekends to cover 'graveyard shifts' as an out-of-vision announcer, both on BBC North TV and radio. I was intrigued. As a career actor the out-of-vision element appealed to me inasmuch as it wouldn't identify me and compromise any 'visible' television acting work that might come my way.

There were certain new skills to master, of course: the ability to write concise 'sound-bites' that were both appetising and informative, and the ability to handle exacting time-constraints, i.e. to have a mental stop-watch ticking in my head. Quite apart from making live announcements there was a rather fearsome self-operated sound and vision mixer to operate while doing so. This appeared on first sight to be a bewildering array of faders and buttons that allowed one to opt in or out of the main network broadcast from London. Scary. Effectively one could be announcing 'live' while listening to talkback or countdowns on headphones, vision mixing, and – all-importantly – keeping a weather eye on the remorseless studio clock. A broadcaster's equivalent, perhaps, of plate-spinning or rubbing your tummy while patting your head. There was a further finesse: after 9.30 in the evenings when the 'BBC North' Duty Office closed for the day, all the enquiries or complaint calls would be routed through to the presentation suite, so one was additionally a kind of acting Duty Officer, noting calls down in the Duty Log.

I cannot tell you how extraordinary I felt answering my first call. I was asked the simple question 'are you the BBC?' and, suddenly imbued with a sense of Reithian responsibility, I was compelled to say 'yes'. Some calls were easier to deal with than others; when an elderly lady phoned to ask if the BBC could send a man to her home I discovered it was because her TV set had just gone on the blink. Needless to say I referred her to a TV repair shop in her locality.

Another call was distinctly bizarre: against a background of very noisy pub chatter a slurred voice told me that he'd got a bet on. Was this tune from Handel's Messiah? He hummed something I recognized as the trumpet voluntary by Jeremiah Clarke. I expressed my personal opinion about the tune, and the caller hung up noisily after a few choice words of disgust. Thanks to the ruddy BBC he'd obviously lost his pub bet. The following day I explained the situation to my superiors, pointing out that I'd actually written the notes he'd hummed on a stave I had scribbled in the Log Book. I was 'carpeted' gently for not having cleared composer attributions properly to accord with 'current BBC thinking'. Heavens, the trumpet tune, although originally ascribed to Clarke, might really have been written by Henry Purcell! Had I not checked?

Ah, 'BBC thinking', forsooth!

Despite this baptism of fire in Manchester as an invisible broadcaster I greatly valued this second-string to my bow, and I went on subsequently to pick up further freelance work as an out-of-vision presentation 'voice' with the BBC in London, and subsequently with Channel 4.

At the time of my early forays up to BBC North, however, I was aware that unless I took some drastic action I was likely to lose Judy to a permanent career in Rome. I had waited for her return for a whole year and had even taken a brief holiday in Italy to join her. What did I want to do? What did she want to do? Clearly I was at an emotional crossroads, as I believe she was herself. I am not overly assertive by nature but the force of a telephone conversation I had with her convinced us both that we were better together in our own company than without it and that, eventually, we should plan to tie the knot. To which end she herself rejoined her former employer, the BBC, to work as a production assistant, while all I could offer her in the way of security was the uncertainty of employment as an actor – boosted occasionally by short spells of freelance voice work. We rented a small flat together in Ealing.

PLAZA SUITE

By this time I was ready to leave the apron-strings of my first agent. She had managed to secure work for me in the past, but mainly in terms of what I'd call 'afterthought' casting, i.e. she would wait until the main parts were settled and generally only then push her clients forward to fill the gaps.

Max Kester, my new agent, had been a notable film and television writer in his day. He was well connected to 'old-school' London theatrical contacts and he certainly seemed to me to have a less restricted outlook than I'd been used to.

I was not disappointed.

Before long he suggested me for a couple of cameo parts in Neil Simon's comedy 'Plaza Suite', a play that had had some success on Broadway and which was now to be mounted in the West End's Lyric Theatre, with Paul Rogers and Rosemary Harris as the stars.

'Plaza Suite' is in fact a suite of three separate one-act plays, all of which are set in Suite 619 of New York's Plaza Hotel and which are basically vehicles for the two 'star' performers. I myself was cast as the hotel bell-hop in the first play and a bridegroom in the third play: I had to persuade my reluctant bride to release herself from the bathroom in which she had locked herself in order to gain sanctuary from her bickering parents.

During the run of 'Plaza Suite', on August 2nd 1969, I became a bridegroom in real life. Judy and I were married in Kensington that day.

I had suggested to her beforehand that as a cost-saving exercise I could ask the theatre if I could be married wearing the morning suit I sported as the bridegroom in Act 3.

Quite rightly Judy was having none of it. Our own wedding was real, not a piece of theatre.

I trailed off dutifully to Moss Bros.

There was no possible cover for my absence from the theatre on the day itself. My 'understudy' was actually the deputy stage manager and, his being over six feet tall, he wouldn't have been able to squeeze himself into costumes designed for an actor only five feet seven inches in height. There was no alternative, and I had to play both a matinée and an evening performance on my wedding day.

My clergyman father performed the ceremony assisted by my clergyman uncle, and my brother-in-law (a music examiner) was in charge of the music. The poor Vicar of St. Mary's Church in the Little Boltons, Kensington where the ceremony took place, might well have considered the event somewhat of a stitch-up, he himself being relatively sidelined as reader of a couple of suitable prayers.

I had to rush away from the guests at the wedding reception in Kensington to get to the theatre in time for the afternoon's performance and both Judy, our parents, and a posse of wedding guests came along eventually to see the evening show which perhaps understandably was more 'relaxed' than usual, the management having laid on generous quantities of Champagne backstage.

My new mother-in-law, sitting helpless with laughter in the stalls, turned to Judy and said 'Is it always like this, this show?' Judy confirmed that it certainly wasn't.

By the same token, of course, I had to be back at the theatre for Monday night's performance! The honeymoon my new wife and I enjoyed at a 'heritage' hotel in Sussex was understandably brief. It rained solidly throughout the weekend.

We chose to stay indoors.

At this time Judy's job at the BBC was as production assistant on 'Blue Peter', so the London Evening Standard's headline on an inside column: 'Blue Peter Girl Weds', was attractively misleading to readers expecting news about one of the programme's presenters.

* * *

SITCOMS

I may well be basking in nostalgia, but it seemed to me that the 1970s and early 80s were the golden age of British television sitcom. There were certainly plenty of them around at the time. Some have remained evergreen classics: 'Dad's Army', 'Porridge', 'Open All Hours', 'Steptoe and Son', 'Only Fools and Horses' and 'The Good Life' amongst them. It was my own good fortune to feature in 'Comedy Playhouse': 'Marry the Girls'; 'Dad's Army', 'Sorry', 'My Wife Next Door', 'Rings on their Fingers' and 'Allo 'Allo' – to name but a few shows across those years.

I am particularly proud to have appeared in an episode of 'Dad's Army'. At the time the 'Sons of the Sea' episode was recorded (1969) I doubt very much that any of the platoon, or David Croft and Jimmy Perry its creators, imagined that the series would achieve such an iconic status in the years to come. It was a classic 'gang show' and as such had brilliantly-written if predictably formulaic, foundations.

I was cast as a regular soldier, a simple 'squaddie' guarding a dockside with a colleague (a RADA and Frinton contemporary of mine, Jonathan Holt). My own part may have been brief, but at least I had the distinction of uttering the crucial plot line on which the story turned.

The BBC back-room staff, as ever, were meticulous in getting the period details right. A week before rehearsals started I was summoned to the hair and make-up department and given the statutory No.1

haircut – a scalping! Judy was shocked to see the result on my return home; we'd not long been married at the time and I guess she wanted me to have hair she could get hold of.

However, later in the week I was detailed to return to the BBC for a costume fitting. Along with my khaki uniform I was kitted out with a woolly balaclava helmet to be worn underneath my tin hat. One could have looked for my regulation military haircut in vain! All anyone could see of me was my swathed face peeping out from its coverings. I guess a little inter-departmental liaison beforehand at the BBC wouldn't have come amiss!

I now regard having worked with the original 'Dad's Army' cast as a great privilege. Needless to say the older members of the Walmington-on-Sea platoon had wartime service backgrounds of their own in a few cases.

Arthur Lowe was predictably brusque in real life, though his range as a brilliant comedy actor went way beyond his celebrated Captain Mainwaring. Additionally, I reckon he was one of the best stage 'drunk' performers I've seen anywhere. John le Mesurier, beyond playing the unworldly Sergeant Wilson, was equally a 'national treasure' both as a fine comedy and also a serious actor.

I discovered pretty quickly that playing television comedy in front of a live studio audience involved the problem of a double perspective. Who is the audience to be played to? Does one time one's laughs from the reactions of the studio audience alone, or does one play to the cameras and to the watching viewers beyond? The television performance is a 'one-off' in any case, but the laughs from the studio audience who are often distracted by extraneous factors or have only a partial view of the studio floor cannot be relied on as safe indicators for timing one's lines. Needless to say the skill in mastering this hybrid technique had been well mastered by the 'old-hands' of the 'Dad's Army' platoon.

FLINT

'Plaza Suite' closed after a run of about nine months and my agent, having set me adrift in a welter of supporting parts in TV sitcoms, was once again keen to keep me visible in the West End. He suggested my name to director Christopher Morahan who was then casting a new play, 'Flint' by David Mercer, an author who was then very much in the public eye. The part on offer was that of a prissy young clergyman, curate to Ossian Flint, an anarchic elderly vicar.

The play itself was effectively a dark comedy and was the author's broadside on what he saw as the obsolescence of inherited institutions such as the Church.

The deliciously subversive vicar Ossian Flint, played by Michael Hordern, is, according to the curate, 'a demented old man raving in an empty church about matters which are the province of the Devil rather than God.'

A strong cast included Vivien Merchant (whose then husband Harold Pinter was a member of the production triumvirate); Julia Foster; Moira Redmond; James Grout and Nicholas Clay.

Although the play attracted critical and public acclaim at the time, its run at the Criterion Theatre was possibly shorter that we all had hoped.

Michael Hordern in particular was tireless in reaching for his character. One might have well considered his performance on the first night as 'perfection', but during the course of the run it grew steadily in stature. He was like a terrier gnawing at a bone to extract every last vestige of depth and flavour out of it.

There was an occasion – just one- when a scene I played with him seemed a bit odder than usual. He was looking at me rather strangely, and I couldn't quite make out why. At the end of the scene I returned to my shared dressing room when my colleague leapt in alarm at the sight of me. I had been wearing a black cassock for the scene, but sitting quietly on my shoulder throughout, obviously enjoying its fifteen minutes of West End stage fame, was a large black cockroach! Mercifully I had been quite oblivious of it ... not so Michael, obviously.

The Criterion Theatre's dressing rooms are in fact underground, and one has to bear in mind that London's theatre-land is also restaurant-land, where the creatures are more than plentiful.

At the time, the Criterion Theatre boasted the oldest stage door-keeper in the business: Harry. Harry was like an overworked trap-door spider. No one crossed the threshold without being challenged for his or her right of access. One day, as part of the production consortium, Harold Pinter appeared at the stage door only to be halted in his tracks. 'Harry' he said,

'You must learn to recognize me ... I keep coming here. I'm part of the Management.' Harry was having none of it.

'What do you want? You can't go backstage, the curtain is up.' A patient Harold Pinter explained,

'I've only come to see my wife, Harry. She's in the play.'

'Who's that then?'

'Vivien Merchant'.

'Well why didn't you say you were Mr Merchant in the first place?' retorted Harry. 'Then I'd have let you in.'

'Flint' ran successfully for about four months in town, and by the end of the run both Judy and I felt the time had come for us to settle down in a place we could call our own. We were beginning to burst out of our tiny flat as it was. Ealing had proved to be a pleasant borough in which to live, and we found a small terraced house about a mile away that seemed ideal for our needs. As an actor I was a little doubtful that we would get a mortgage. I assumed the Building Society might well take the view that my own income was too unreliable, and consider their financial risk in taking us on as too high. I know at the time we were looking at a mortgage of around £5,000 which figure nowadays seems laughable.

I needn't have worried. Judy's regular employment with the BBC and 'Blue Peter' might have carried the day against the 'feast and famine' of my own more insecure career.

I do remember, though, that the local Estate Agent handling the property at the time took exception to dealing with Judy in my absence simply on the ground that she was a woman, even though she would be joint mortgagee.

Funny how little details stick.

COMMERCIALS

When otherwise 'resting' as an actor – and I had a fair bit of experience in the gentle art of being out of work, it was often a financial Godsend to be cast in a TV or film commercial. Early in my career there were still vestiges of general disapproval about engaging in such infra dig enterprises. High-minded thespians used to consider work in commercials as a prostitution of one's art, and that if one had any integrity worth the name one stayed clear of them altogether. At the time work of this kind began to come my way, the climate of stuffy disapproval was easing considerably and – if one was lucky enough to appear in a commercial that had been cut in various different ways to be shown across a range of domestic TV regions there could be considerable financial rewards in repeat fees.

Actor Richard Briers of 'The Good Life' fame paid tribute to the fact that by voicing just one coffee commercial alone he was financially enabled to play King Lear for Kenneth Branagh's Renaissance Theatre Company, which otherwise he would not have been able to afford to do.

Featuring in commercials for the domestic market on British television was not the only work of this kind available, there were also opportunities to film abroad. Apparently foreign clients not only admired the on-screen naturalism of British actors but also found us relatively cheap to employ!

Nowadays Equity has probably tightened up the rules regarding its members' work in commercials overseas. Previously, even taking into account the frills of being flown to and returned from our destination 'club class' and being put up in a decent hotel, we were cost-effective because we were subject to a buy-out clause. There was obviously no effective way of policing repeat fees and residual payments for commercials made and shown abroad.

British commercial appearances aside, in my 'continental' career I have ostensibly been a German (twice), a Dutchman (twice), a Spaniard, an Italian, a Frenchman and a Francophone Swiss.

Perhaps my most memorable commercial shoot was for German television, though filmed in England by director Bob Brooks.

The product was 'Lifebuoy' soap and the scene was one of intimate domesticity.

Picture the scene: the commercial begins with a close-up shot of the bar of soap. My hand now comes into shot reaching downwards for it, lifting the soap aloft to reveal me sitting in a bath, soaping myself with it.

So far so good. The camera then pulls out a little whereupon my 'wife' appears, sitting at the other end of the bath. I pass her the soap and we share the joy of soaping ourselves! Decorum is (just) preserved as everything is being shot at bath-rim level.

However, the representative from the advertising agency in Munich who is sitting with the director is not happy with my partner's appearance. She doesn't seem to him to be ... erm ... Germanic enough. Could she not possibly have a little more 'uplift' in the chest area?

There is a lengthy break for discussion in the studio while both I and my 'wife' sit in a steadily-cooling bath, awaiting the outcome. A member of the studio crew has a bright idea: could not a couple of strips of adhesive-backed camera tape be applied strategically onto my 'wife's body in order to raise her forward profile to more acceptable Teutonic proportions?

My 'wife' is not sure, but she is persuaded, reluctantly, and the deed is done. Just as shooting recommenced I could see that my partner was already in considerable distress. The adhesive on the rough-and-ready camera tape had reacted violently with her delicate bare skin, and she was in agony! Not the usual kind of industrial injury, I suspect, and no further progress seemed possible. But wait! My 'wife' (No.1) is paid off at lunchtime with profuse apologies, and a quick re-cast for 'wife' (No.2) is put in place. She arrives within the half hour, and is seen to be everything ... more than everything ... the German advertising man seems to require, although this means we have to start shooting again from scratch.

Around teatime the German agency man belatedly spots a new problem, however. I am not wearing a wedding ring! A fatal flaw! This would be customary in continental Europe hence the commercial as shot so far is un-broadcastable. A ring of some kind is quickly borrowed from one of the studio crew and, guess what, we start all over again!

You may be well aware of what overstaying in a bath can do to the skin: my 'wife' and I emerged from our shared tub at the end of an extra-long day looking like two wrinkled prunes!

I think, no, I know, that the most demanding day's work I have ever done on a commercial was on a shoot in Madrid for a Spanish insurance company. I was told in advance that I would have to fill forty seconds of fluent Spanish dialogue in close-up directly to camera.

As I don't happen to speak Spanish you may rightly wonder why I was cast for the job in the first place, but the advertising agency preferred to have northern European-type actors rather than indigenous ones because, seemingly, they carried more authority.

My voice would be dubbed by a Spanish voiceover artist in post-production in any case. This was all very well, but I would have to deliver the dialogue correctly so that his voice could be properly lip-synchronized. My agent strove unsuccessfully to obtain a script in advance of my flying out to Madrid, and needless to say I was becoming ever more concerned about having time to learn my speech. At the Spanish end of the line mañana seemed to be the watchword. The production company seemed unduly relaxed about providing the necessary information. Finally, on my eventual arrival in Madrid, a cassette tape of the dialogue was provided for me – but there was still no script! There was nothing for it: I would have to spend the night trying to get at least the sounds of what I would be saying into my head if, alas, not the sense. The recording, rather than being helpful, was a disaster. It sounded as if it had been made by a Spaniard who was obviously suffering from a heavy cold.

Equally he seemed to have recorded the dialogue at a room's distance from the microphone. A nightmare!

I spent a sleepless night in my hotel bedroom trying to get the sounds locked into my head, timing them religiously to forty seconds, in dread meanwhile of the following morning's filming session. Should I have worried? I was driven to the studios from my hotel at daybreak and introduced to the director. He was charming but admitted that there was just a little change. Nothing much.

My heart sank.

'We do not now shoot forty seconds' he said, 'we have now thirty seconds'. Good news? I hardly thought so.

Now I didn't know which parts of my barely-learned dialogue would have to be truncated. Neither did I know the sense of the dialogue that was going to have to be cut. The director waved my anxieties away.

'Don't worry', he said, 'We keep all the dialogue as it is. All we need you to do is to speak your lines so very much faster'.

Foolishly I once accepted work on a commercial for the Furniture Show at Earl's Court where the brief storyline featured two ragged castaways who were both anticipating the event and discussing where their new furniture might go aboard their tiny raft. A weak joke, perhaps, but hardly a joke at all when it came to filming. There was a raft, certainly, and the slender young girl who was my partner and I were both skimpily dressed in ragged cheesecloth tops and threadbare jeans in true castaway fashion, but the commercial was shot just off the coast of Eastbourne in the choppy English Channel in the teeth of a howling November gale! Both the girl and I hung on grimly as the raft, raked by an icy wind, teetered about in the choppy sea.

We both nearly died of cold, and all for a fifteen-second shot of ourselves afloat and well-nigh unrecognizable in the far distance! Cardboard cut-out figures would have served just as well.

I was somewhat surprised when I first heard the lengths to which advertising companies could sometimes go in order to film commercials. In the days when I was playing furry creatures in 'Toad of Toad Hall', actor Richard Goolden recounted the story that he had once been cast in a commercial for Gale's Honey simply as an old man asleep on a hammock in a quintessentially English summer garden, bees buzzing and butterflies fluttering around the lupins and hollyhocks in front of a rustic thatched cottage. Shortly after securing the job, and to his great surprise, a dispatch-rider arrived at his house bearing a set of air-tickets.

'What's all this?' he asked.

'Its your airline tickets'. Dickie was astonished.

'What for?'

'Alicante', came the reply.

'They are for your commercial. I hope your passport's in order'.

Fortunately it was, and he was astonished to find on his arrival at the location that the Spanish crew had not only built the frontage of a thatched English cottage but had also landscaped a complete flowery cottage-style garden around it and, on the newly-laid lawn, had replanted two mature trees at a hammock's distance apart - a not inconsiderable expense - and all to secure the all-important radiant sunshine that filming in the English Cotswolds simply couldn't guarantee.

Recognized celebrities who feature in commercials are understandably bought-out at a handsome fee, their appearance being seen as their personal endorsement of the product in question. Maybe 'they're worth it'.

For the mass of middle-range relatively unidentified actors such as myself it was usually a matter of attending an audition.

Auditions? Sometimes these were rather more like cattle markets. Agents all over town would submit artistes (regardless sometimes of their suitability) and one would take one's turn in what seemed to be a never-ending queue. There were occasions when the director filming the commercial would ask one to perform a piece of improvisation on the spot. Sometimes it was rather obvious that the production team were actually looking for ideas off the actors' backs, cost-free. One wonders somewhat cynically how many scenarios for commercials have been created this way across a day's auditioning schedule.

It was no great comfort to be told that in terms of primary research, test videos, focus group meetings, agency salaries during consultation, and the whole paraphernalia of getting the show on the road, the actors' share in fees often worked out at around 1% of the budget for the commercial as a whole.

One casting session had serious implications for me in later life. I don't even remember the product in question but the sight-joke was that of small man dancing with huge overweight lady. You'll have anticipated my own role in this scenario, I suspect. However, during the audition at the Pineapple Dance Studios in Covent Garden, my cumbersome partner accidentally missed her footing and fell on top of me. I put my arm out to break my heavy fall, and apart from our joint shock both my partner and I seemed to have survived without further injury. The following day my right hand began to throb rather painfully, though no bruising or broken skin was visible. The next day I was beginning to feel a bit off-colour and the throbbing in my hand persisted rather worryingly. It was only when red lines began to appear, running up my right arm, that I realised that there was something seriously wrong.

Clearly, my hand had somehow become infected, and a speedy trip to hospital confirmed this to be the case, the localised infection site being dealt with surgically as a matter of urgency.

By this time, however, the infection had already spread up my arm and had now reached a valve in my heart. This resulted in my contracting bacterial endocarditis, a rather more life-threatening condition which required hospitalization for a month and which affected my heart and health thereafter – to which continuing story I shall return later.

DON'T START WITHOUT ME

Beyond the occasional diversions of commercials there was yet another opportunity for work in the West End! The comedy four-hander 'Don't Start Without Me' by Joyce Rayburn had opened at the Garrick Theatre in 1971 starring Paul Daneman, Jan Waters,

Lucy Fleming and Brian Cox. Both Lucy Fleming and Brian Cox had 'get-out' clauses in their contracts which permitted them to leave the show mid-stream, so to speak, so their parts were to be recast. Liz Bamber and I took over from them for the remainder of the play's run. As the hapless nerdy 'Norman' I remember I wore a thick Arran sweater that Judy had knitted for me when we were first engaged which by this time had stretched sufficiently to suggest a certain comedic potential. She let me wear it, but in the event I am not sure she was overly happy to let her loving handiwork feature as comedy costume.

All good things come to an end, including that particular play, and as all freelancers may recognize, one has to snatch opportunities for a holiday when one can. Judy and I headed off to the Loire valley for a little autumnal magic. We both adored the region and we particularly remember our visit to the fairytale Château of Chenonceaux, a breathtakingly beautiful vision among the trees, burnished by the sunlight of a golden afternoon. No wonder we were astonished to hear the lady sitting behind us in our coach complain 'I don't know why our driver's bothered to take us here. I can't see any shops.'

There was gastronomic beauty along the Loire too. We ate incomparably well. Neither of us realised at the time that Judy was eating for two! She was in the earliest stages of pregnancy and obviously would have to leave work at some stage. With new family commitments ahead I was more than keen to pick up another longer-term commitment as an actor, no matter how many *ad hoc* freelance voice-work contracts for BBC presentation might – or might not - turn up.

RAINBOW

I am not sure now how the invitation came about, but shortly after we had returned from our trip along the Loire I was put forward to audition for a character in a brand new series Thames TV were producing called 'Rainbow'.

'Rainbow', was a daytime show aimed specifically at the under-fives, and the character I was pencilled for was Bungle Bear ... effectively the representative 'child' who would join in songs and games with the show's puppets and interact with and learn from the show's presenter, David Cook.

The producer, Pamela Lonsdale, accepted me for the part, but as I left her office at Teddington studios I had second thoughts. I wondered to myself if I actually wanted to hide away from my profession inside a bear costume across (initially) a year's contract.

I put my doubts aside. My new responsibility as the sole family breadwinner should not be overlooked, especially as a job on a television series offered the promise of a better fee than the theatre could provide.

The stylised bear costume I was to wear as Bungle was custom-made and had to look relatively believable as a bear, and Thames TV had commissioned the designer who had created the wonderful animal costumes for the Royal Ballet's production of 'Tales of Beatrix Potter' to design it. I hadn't expected to be called in specially to model for the bear's mask, but as I was to sport a bear's head for the foreseeable future it was an advantage to have something to wear that was relatively comfortable. I hadn't anticipated what was to follow.

I had a plaster-cast taken of my face. This was a somewhat alarming procedure which started with having my face greased, then being given two breathing straws to stick up my nostrils, and finally having my face liberally covered with plaster of Paris which had to stay glued to me, warming up, until it set! Quite honestly I think I'd have preferred a heavy session with the dentist.

No matter, the bear's head was duly delivered to the studio and it proved a reasonably comfortable fit, which was just as well after the trouble that had been taken to have it fashioned specially for me. There was an unforeseen practical difficulty, though. Bungle's eyes were not set quite in front of my own, which meant that when wearing the head I was partially-sighted and very likely to break the second rule of coarse acting: 'don't bump into the furniture'.

The 'Rainbow' schedule was quite demanding. We rehearsed and recorded three shows a week. I could certainly have recommended my experience while in the studio as Bungle to anyone trying to slim. Under the hot bright lights of Teddington's smallest studio the temperature inside my furry costume was fearsome.

Needless to say, my character was supposed to be bouncily energetic and enthusiastic, a heat-inducing physical process in itself. I won't describe too graphically how damp I became during studio sessions, save to say that in order to get through each day's recording I had to be issued with salt tablets to prevent me from collapsing altogether.

After my year's incarceration inside the skin of Bungle, during which time our son Guy was born, I felt not only that I had slimmed down to the dimensions of a Giacometti sculpture, but also that it was high time for me to be 'visible' once again as an actor. The mantle of Bungle, so to speak, now fell on an actor called Stanley Bates who was physically smaller than I, and I half-suspected that Thames TV was looking only for replacement actors who were already pre-shrunk. I hoped that the costume he was to have inherited had been given a thorough dry-clean at the end of the show's first season, but apparently a new and rather more cuddly one had been commissioned in the old one's place.

Equally, David Cook retired from the show, eventually to establish for himself a notable career as a novelist and writer. I dare not claim the entire credit for replacing David. I certainly introduced my old Dundee 'Rep colleague Geoffrey Hayes to 'Rainbow's producer, Pamela Lonsdale, and the rest, as they say, is history.

Geoffrey remained as the show's presenter for several years thereafter. Me? Let's say I escaped as I was about to reach vanishing point! Though, looking back, I pay tribute to the skill and patience of David Cook as the on-screen father figure of the first series of 'Rainbow' and equally to the skills of the puppeteers whose creations of the pink hippo 'George' and the – whatever he was - 'Zippy', plus several other guest puppets, whose characters were brought to life vocally by the matchless Peter Hawkins and Roy Skelton.

'WE'LL LET YOU KNOW…'

I seem to remember that the year I left 'Rainbow' was alive with auditions of various kinds as I felt the need to get my face seen about the place following my spell of well-paid furry anonymity.

Auditions are part and parcel of a working actor's life, their importance being such that there is now a thriving sub-industry run by drama teachers or even 'resting' actors offering coaching in 'audition technique'.

This is obviously a second cousin to the industry that grooms political high-flyers and others requiring to achieve the best impact possible on screen and elsewhere.

In the world of the theatre there is the apocryphal story of the aspiring actress on Broadway who had spent her life auditioning, and never missed any opportunity of being seen for a show. One day, we are told, she was actually offered a part. 'Oh no', she said, 'I don't want to take it. I just do auditions'.

At about this time Michael Crawford was stepping down from 'No Sex, Please, We're British' in the West End, and I was invited to see his performance which turned out to be one of the most athletic tours de force I'd seen anywhere. I duly turned up for the audition with the author and the director a couple of days later, but although I had prepared well and had a good feeling for the part it was not to be.

I don't want to parade my deficiencies too heavily, but I well recall three notable occasions when I left an audition or job interview with the certainty that I hadn't got the part on offer: I once auditioned for a part in a musical at Drury Lane where the stage at the Theatre Royal is one of the widest in London.

I was a non-starter even before I started out. I had hardly taken more than four or five paces across the stage in my bid to perform the song I had prepared when Jerome Robbins, the show's director, called out from the stalls 'Thank you, that's all!' So I just walked straight across what seemed miles of floor space to the wings the other side ... and home!

As a result of writing 'work' letters I eventually obtained an interview with a very grand casting lady at Associated-Rediffusion Television at Kingsway House, Holborn. She had graciously deigned to see me having sent me a letter which started 'In view of your understandable persistence...'

Not the best omen, perhaps.

An appointment was duly made, and I was ushered into her plush office to find her rearranging an enormous vase of flowers, possibly from Mayfair's Moyses Stevens, on her desk. She invited me to sit down, then she subtly engineered the vase between herself and me so that she had no view of me whatsoever.

The interview itself was pleasant enough, if brief, but the negative outcome was hardly surprising. Maybe had she auditioned the flowers they'd have got the part. They were exquisite.

The third occasion was a casting for a film part with director Woody Allen. I cannot now remember which film it might have been, but as I wasn't cast in it, it is of no consequence. I was called to meet him at his suite in the Dorchester Hotel.

On my arrival I was warmly greeted by his secretary and shown up to the suite where I expected to meet the director. The secretary sat me down and told me about the film, and it was only when I was leaving that I noticed that Woody Allen had been standing in a far corner of the room with his back turned, looking rather shyly out of the window, absorbed in thought.

I can't say I made as much of an impression on him as some of his film work has made on me, but, as with all auditions, 'nothing ventured, nothing gained'.

On a visit home some years earlier I plucked up courage to 'cold-call' Clive Perry, the director of Leicester's Phoenix Theatre, to try my luck in having a 'general audition' rather than for any specific part he might have been thinking of casting at the time.

He kindly consented to see me, but at the time I called at the theatre the main stage was in use for rehearsals so he ushered me into one of the dressing rooms, plonked himself down on a chair, and got me to start.

To my horror I found myself auditioning not only for him but reflectively for myself - my sternest judge. The wall behind him was ceiling-to-floor mirror glass! Never had I ever auditioned so self-consciously as on that occasion. He didn't offer me a part subsequently, and in the circumstances I don't think I would have offered myself one either.

There is nothing more unsettling than being brought face to face with the inadequacies of one's own performance while performing!

DOGGED BY DR WHO

The lengthy history of myself and Doctor Who really starts in 1977, and believe it or not I didn't even have to audition!

I had worked with the director Derrick Goodwin on several occasions, notably at Nottingham Repertory Theatre, and I ran into him quite accidentally one evening in Ealing at 'The Kent', my local pub at the time. Derrick happened to be there because he had just finished a day's filming on 'Z-Cars' which had been shot in the locality and was taking the opportunity to wind down.

He was his normal effusive self, and told me that now he'd seen me again he might have something in mind for me to play. Now normally when directors come out with that kind of 'spiel' one suspends belief, an insurance born of all-too-frequent experience... but no, he asked if I had ever watched 'Doctor Who'? I admitted that I had.

He wouldn't say any more about it, or give hints or clues, but told me that he was scheduled to direct one of the storylines and that I might possibly expect to hear something from the BBC within a week or two. True to his word I received a call from my agent at the end of the following week informing me that the BBC wanted to know if I would be interested in playing not one but two parts in the forthcoming storyline of Doctor Who! This was exciting enough, but I asked my agent what the parts were.

'Ah, that's the funny thing, John' he said. 'One is the voice of a virus – and the other is the voice of a tin dog! What do you think?'

Regardless of the offer of paid work, once again I confess that I was in two minds about it. Had I earned myself a reputation, I wondered, by pigeonholing myself into the slot marked 'voice artiste' at the expense of anything else. My agent assured me that there was little to lose: the part of K9 had been written-in for one storyline only, and in any case my engagement would be properly as an actor rather than a voiceover provider 'phoning-in' the dialogue from the sidelines. The rest you may know. Over thirty years onwards K9 is still following me at heel!

Having shown a passing interest to my agent, a meeting was arranged for me with producer Graham Williams. He explained that the character was a dog-shaped robot which had not only encyclopaedic recall of facts, figures and parameters of risk, but also considerable defensive capability.

K9 was not the Doctor's creature but had been built by a 'Professor Marius', the director of a space biological foundation, as a canine personal assistant.

'He is only featuring in one storyline' Graham apologised, 'and unfortunately the model we're making of him hasn't yet been built, but let me show you some blueprints of what the character will look like.'

I wondered momentarily if he was going to ask me to get inside it, as K9 seemed to have been designed to be quite a size! Fortunately not. The module would be radio-controlled much in the same way as applied to model aircraft, and I myself wouldn't be required to operate it, simply to be its voice and character throughout the story.

Graham asked what kind of a voice I might use, based on what I'd seen of the blueprints. I remembered Ken Russell's film 'Billion Dollar Brain', made a decade earlier, where a massive computer spits out disconnected words – a sound equivalent of the poison-pen letter that uses words hacked out from newspaper cuttings, pasted to form sentences. We both discarded this idea pretty swiftly as too lumbering and unmodulated, particularly as K9 might have to deliver some rapid-fire repartee.

On leaving Graham's office I promised to go home and put down some 'try-out' voices on tape for him to listen to and I hoped, having done that, I might be considered for the job.

Having sent my sample voices to him I sat down at home and waited for a response. A fortnight later I received a panic call from the Doctor Who office: Graham's secretary rang to inquire if I had actually accepted the job! I had wrongly assumed that I was just one of a long queue of actors who had been seen for the part and didn't realise that at the time I met him it had been mine for the taking.

I think my own memory of my days in mainstream Doctor Who has become a little moth-eaten in places, partly because of the kind of 'slate-clearing' that regular actors in a series habitually apply as one storyline succeeds another. In any case, I can bypass the varied history of K9 and the detailed minutiae of all the stories in which the character featured as they can easily be accessed on the web, which is certainly a relief to my typing fingers.

I used to be amazed by the historians amongst the Doctor Who fan base whose intimate knowledge of every aspect of the series, both classic and modern, is now charted and updated for posterity, but perhaps I am less surprised nowadays as so much is now instantly reviewable at the touch of a mouse-click. Is there yet a Chair in Doctor Who Studies at some outlying university? It wouldn't surprise me in the least.

Insofar as any series based on science-fantasy is concerned I know the most important moment of rehearsals is the initial read-through with all the cast. Only then do you get to meet everybody, and only then do you have a chance to hear the storyline read through from start to finish. What follows thereafter is a jig-saw rehearsal schedule compromised by the requirements of the studio sets, location filming and, in some cases, actors' availability. The next time the whole piece can be seen in its entirety is, of course, on transmission itself.

I learned to my disappointment on that first rehearsal day that the K9 module was still in preparation and would not be available until the recording day itself. This set-back, however, turned out to be a wonderful blessing in disguise. Bearing in mind that I had been engaged as an actor and not simply as a 'voice', I volunteered to run around the rehearsal room floor being K9.

At least the other actors could see where K9 was supposed to be travelling at any point of time, but far more importantly it set up a valuable dynamic relationship between the character and those with whom he would subsequently interact, chiefly Tom Baker as The Doctor. This was a wonderful building block which was to support us both throughout our time together on the series.

Additionally it was crucial when put to the test of having the 'real' K9 on the studio floor, when it was no wonder that Tom's ideal was to have had me running around dressed as a dog rather than having to cope, as we both did, with a manifestly unreliable and inexpressive machine. Tom's dislike for the inanimate K9 was firmly rooted and a matter of record, nonetheless in his autobiography 'Who on Earth is Tom Baker?' he acknowledges that 'John Leeson, (who) if he had been allowed to be a dog could have been immortal'.

Ah, if only!

There is no doubt that the lumbering K9 module was a pain, both in the studios and on location. Nigel Brackley, his operator at the time and, subsequently, Mat Irvine, constantly had to step in to administer running repairs, replacing or adjusting belt drives etc. More worryingly, the delays in getting K9 going were eating into valuable studio time.

At the studio recordings for K9's debut story 'The Invisible Enemy' the radio signals that were being fed to K9 were on a frequency that disturbed the studio cameras. Whenever my alter ego trundled noisily into shot the cameras simply snowed up! Equally K9 was extremely heavy and almost fatally under-powered. Were he to have run up to as much as a matchstick on the studio floor he would have stalled, and wherever there was a doorframe with a tie-bar across the floor through which he had to pass, the recording had to be paused while he was carried bodily over the threshold, when a camera shot would pick him up again the other side, as if having come through the doorway under his own steam. (I remember that shortly after 'The

Invisible Enemy' was broadcast I received a very heavy envelope through my letterbox at home on which I had to pay hefty excess postage: a child had 'invented' K9's birthday, and had sent a card and a handful of ball-bearings as a present 'to make him go faster'.)

Lack of speed aside, whenever a two-shot of close conversation between The Doctor and K9 was required Tom would have to accommodate the camera shot by going down on one knee to talk to him. Inelegant at best, I thought, and I dare say Tom's own thoughts on having to oblige were a great deal darker.

I, meanwhile, was tasked with feeding in K9's dialogue 'live' on a sports lip-mike, having been banished to the far end of the studio where I sat watching the robot's halting and seemingly drunken progress on a monitor screen.

It was ridiculous, of course, but I began to feel terribly guilty. At least I had solidified the character in rehearsal, and now – of all the times – the physical K9 was not only subverting all my efforts but wasting valuable time.

I consoled myself with the thought that with all the difficulties he was causing, the production team would be getting rid of him once the end-credits rolled on the current story. It was not to be, however, and Graham Williams sanctioned K9's official status in the ranks of the Doctor's companions thereafter.

There's a sense in which the BBC has to pay a dog licence fee every time K9 is used. It is probably not generally appreciated that copyright in K9 is not vested in the BBC but in Bob Baker and his writing partner Dave Martin (now deceased) who co-wrote 'The Invisible Enemy'. Dave Martin's own dog had apparently been killed in a road accident and K9 was dreamed up as an indestructible imaginary replacement for his pet for the purposes of the story. There is a corollary, of course. I remember that once K9's voice had 'entered the public domain' my agent used to get calls for me to play computer voices on TV commercials. Obviously it appeared to the so-called creative advertising agencies that I was the specialist in robotic or computer voices. I wonder why.

Whereas Dalek voices were heavily treated, my own as K9 was generally left alone. Once I had characterised it, it did exactly what it says on the tin, so to speak, though I think originally the BBC's duty sound engineer Mike McCarthy ran it through a ring modulator simply to make it sound a bit tinnier than it does naturally.

The question on everyone's lips whenever I turned up at a fan gathering in the early days was 'What is it like to work with Tom Baker?' I would often respond with the mischievously evasive answer 'Yes!', and leave it at that – but in truth, despite Tom's reputation for being difficult, I got on extremely well with him.

Admittedly our personalities are as disparate as chalk and cheese, but I think the fact of my having crawled about as K9 on the rehearsal room floor amused Tom greatly. One ignores the truism that 'one should never act with animals or children' at one's peril lest one should be upstaged, but I likened our professional relationship to that of master and servant or, if you want to be Shakespearean about it, King Lear and his fool. At least I could be expressive and reactive in rehearsals whereas the gunmetal-grey robot that eventually appeared on camera was expressionless, able to offer little other than 'what you see is what you get'.

As much as anything else, I tried to carry the sparkiness of the K9 attitude achieved in rehearsals across to the technically compromised studio sessions. In terms purely of scripts, though, one has to accept that there cannot be anything too contentious in robot-speak. K9 didn't have an internal or an emotional life, but there was scope in the writing both then and in subsequent stories for plenty of chutzpah from the character.

Had he not been cut short on occasion by the Doctor he would doubtless have chattered on regardless, with plenty to say for himself.

Although K9 is not a dog, he is recognizably dog-shaped, and I now wonder idly in hindsight just how much of the loyalty I felt towards Tom's Doctor was subconsciously influenced by the relationship of any dog towards its master. Purely on a character basis the writers had conjured up a partnership of equals – K9's pedantic arrogance and perky one-upmanship as a foil to the mercurial and intuitive behaviour of Tom's Time Lord.

Tom Baker's own autobiographical analysis of himself and his complexities speaks for itself.

Likewise, I am all too aware of my own personal foibles, and I suppose my professional attitude in general carries a degree of objectivity with it.

I admit to having a quiet, if slightly distanced empathy with others who are equally if somewhat more elaborately convoluted than myself! Perhaps there's a wider lesson here for me that I shouldn't be so patient. Someone once described me as 'the still centre of the raging storm' – and I've never quite worked out if that was a compliment or a criticism - let alone if it was true.

What I found remarkable in Tom purely as an actor was his combination of mental and physical energy, his ease in striking a metaphorical 'thirteen' rather than twelve – and his quicksilver ability to think imaginatively if somewhat surreally ... virtues that seemed essential in a Time Lord, in which casting he seemed more than ideal.

Much of Tom's bravura seemed to me to hide ancient and painful scars. There was one occasion I recall when Tom didn't show up for rehearsals. He was often to be found in the early hours in sound studios in Soho doing voiceovers, so that was where he was assumed to be. The director rehearsed all the scenes in which Tom was not involved. Time passed. Still no Tom.

Then at about midday the double-doors of the fourth-floor rehearsal room at North Acton burst open, and there he was – beaming all over his face and exclaiming 'So sorry everyone ... I simply couldn't stop crying!'

Equally, Tom's attitude to the character of Leela, the naïve intuitive savage played by the incomparable Louise Jameson is a matter of record in his own autobiography and, as Louise freely admits, the female assistants weren't treated at all well by the hierarchy in those early days. Time has moved on, and I can only hope that today's breed of the Doctor's female assistants are allowed to give as good as they get both on and off-screen.

Particularly for an audience of children, both Tom and I were keen to preserve the magic and to some extent the mystery of the characters we played. Tom's natural bonhomie with young fans was impressive to say the least, whatever his own private attitude to them may have been, and whenever children spotted K9 I made sure I kept myself well in the background - not to break any cherished illusions, let alone cultivate any mistaken suspicions of a ventriloquism act.

Mat Irvine, who has had care and maintenance of the various K9 'bodies' through the years, told me of an occasion when he had taken the K9 module to some public event where I was not able to be present myself, being urged by young fans to 'make him speak, mister. Make him speak!'

We were lucky to have had Robert Holmes as our script editor for 'Invisible Enemy', but occasionally scripts would appear in which Tom was loaded with huge amounts of dialogue that would sink a galleon.

'This is horse-shit!' He would shout. 'Wireless!'

It was not that he particularly minded learning dialogue, but television was a visual medium after all, and this 'baffle-gab' was simply padding, marking time emptily until something happened.

Quite justifiably on one occasion, and where possible, Tom would redistribute chunks of one of his particularly long speeches amongst other players, effectively freeing-up an otherwise static piece of dialogue.

Visually, too, he would ensure that he himself always provided some eye-catching movement at the first frame of every scene in which he appeared – an old trick, but one designed to keep the audience's eye active.

On the studio floor or when filming, his reliance on the cameramen was a constant factor.

'How big am I in frame?' he would ask; he then knew for certain how expansive he could afford to be in long-shot, or how constrained and minimal his movements would have to be in close-up. It is not for me to say how well Tom got on with directors, but I guess he was less dismissive of them than Wilfred Hyde White had been, whose earlier comment on drama schools you may recall.

'Don't talk to me about Directors, dear! They are the most useful people in the theatre. If you ask them nicely they'll help carry your scripts to the car.'

During rehearsals of scenes in which Tom and I were not personally involved we would retire to the side of the room and struggle together to make sense of

'The Times' crossword. It was a matter of honour for us to try and finish it before lunchtime if possible. We were obviously trying to get ourselves in training to match the prowess of the production secretary Gwen Foyle who would always arrive bright and early on the morning of the producer's 'run' with her Times crossword fully completed.

Maybe she took after the notable actress Celia Johnson of 'Brief Encounter' fame. Her own approach to the Times crossword was apparently to sit looking at it for fifteen minutes or so, pondering its complexities, then, taking up her pen, she would fill it all in at one go.

No so Sir John Gielgud, perhaps. An apocryphal story went round to the effect that when sitting with other actors in a green-room waiting his cue to go on stage he would allow himself to be seen working away at his Times crossword, grunting quietly as if having 'eureka' moments of success, to the frustration of his colleagues who were likewise working on their own crosswords. Once he had gone on stage his fellow actors couldn't resist having a peek to see what clues he'd solved that they themselves couldn't yet reach. Apparently he had simply filled in the blanks with complete gobbledygook!

There were occasions when K9 would be involved in scenes shot on location and although my voice would usually be added at a later stage in a dubbing theatre,

I was required to join the rest of the cast and the filming crew as a matter of course.

Effectively I had nothing to do other than to be there, and perhaps utter the odd line or two of K9 dialogue purely as a guide track, to be dubbed at a later stage in the sound edit.

The story 'The Stones of Blood' was filmed around the megalithic circle called the Rollright Stones on the Oxfordshire-Warwickshire borders, and gave rise to the already well-ventilated 'crossword' story...it is one which bears repeating here.

I myself was seated in the front seat of one of the BBC's huge outside broadcast video vans about half a mile away from the actors and film crew. I had been equipped with a microphone and a pair of headphones so that my voice could be relayed to the location and I likewise could hear my cues.

Through the headphones I remember hearing the director Darrol Blake calling out 'take five, everyone — we're going to set up the next shot', and shortly afterwards Tom's voice came through.

'Are you there, John?' he called. I confirmed I could hear him, and my voice must have come through the loudspeakers at his end of the line.

'Have you got your 'Times' crossword with you?' he enquired. I confirmed that I had, and we proceeded to try and crack a few clues together while the rest of the cast had been stood down. What I didn't know at the time and couldn't have seen from my distant spot was what the local villagers watching the filming from the sidelines were witnessing - Tom Baker as The

Doctor sitting down on the grass verge with K9 plonked beside him, and both of them doing 'The Times' crossword together!

The onlookers' suspension of disbelief must have been complete!

There were two very special joys for me on that filming spree: the company of the lovely Susan Engel who played Vivien Fay, and the wonderful Beatrix Lehmann as Professor Rumford.

I had asked Beatrix if she minded my taking some photographs of her on location purely for personal rather than publicity reasons, and she happily agreed. They were a great success – or at least she led me to believe so.

A few days after our return to London and back into rehearsals she approached me one morning bearing a brown paper bag which she thrust into my hands. I wondered what on earth she was offering me. 'This is for you, dear' she said.

'I shan't be needing it again and I'd like you to have it'. My amazement at opening the bag and finding a 1936 Leica camera, complete with its leather case, was overwhelming. I insisted it was far too precious a gift to give to me, let alone for a handful of black-and-white photographs I'd taken of her.

'No dear' she insisted in return. 'It was given to me by an old friend a long time ago – and now I want it to be yours'.

For my part there are times when the words 'thank you' seem poor currency in return for such a generous gift. Both Tom and I wondered if the 'old friend' might have been the actor Ralph Richardson whom she had so greatly admired and loved in her youth.

Beatrix, sadly, is no longer with us. Her work on 'Stones of Blood' was the last television engagement she undertook before she died. I'd like to think that she is aware ... somewhere ... that her camera is now safely in the custody of my film-maker son Guy who has used it to great effect for some of his own personal photographs.

By this time, Louise Jameson had departed as Leela, and the Time Lord Doctor now had a frosty Time Lady companion to contend with.

Romanadvoratrelundar — 'Romana', played by the elegant Mary Tamm. Behind the scenes, Mary was delightfully down to earth and had the driest sense of humour imaginable. She was great fun, a godsend during the longueurs of rehearsals or recording breaks. She was no slouch when it came to solving crossword puzzles, either.

By the beginning of the 1979-80 season of Doctor Who, K9 had become a firmly established companion in the series, but I was beginning to feel increasingly that there was nowhere further that I could take the character. Like the Daleks, Cybermen, Sontarans or whatever else, I feared that K9 was falling into a stereotype which, now established, was incapable of further development. I felt too that the writers were becoming less inventive with his use in the storylines and were beginning to treat K9 rather more like a 'get out of jail' card for the Doctor when in difficulties – another kind of 'sonic screwdriver' perhaps.

I have little doubt, looking back that (if this was the case) it was due as much to the physical limitations of the K9 module in the studio as to any lack of imagination on the writers' part. For my own part, though, I had had a tremendous amount of fun playing K9, I considered, probably rightly at the time, that I should take the opportunity of giving myself greater visual exposure as an actor in the world outside Doctor Who.

I decided to leave, in my own best interests, and not without regret. Needless to say one doesn't take this kind of decision lightly, and I had absolutely no idea whether I would get any further work once I'd flown the comfortable nest. In point of fact I now remember that once I'd left the series I had one of the most work-packed years of my career to date!

My replacement as the voice of K9 was the actor David Brierley. I knew him slightly as I had occasionally shared a platform with him in the past when we had both been seconded into a poetry recital group called 'Matchlight'. David obviously had the unenviable task of following-on from the matrix I'd set, and didn't necessarily deserve the criticism he received in some quarters for developing K9 in his own vocal style.

I understand that the change of voice was explained in the stories as K9 suffering from laryngitis. I never got to see any of David's episodes, but in later years we were both invited to appear at a Doctor Who convention together. We had great fun pretending that we were snippy rivals, and mischievously played up a faux-antipathy towards each other in order to keep the audience amused.

BLAKE'S SEVEN

I wouldn't like to suggest that casting at the BBC was too incestuous, but it may have been a temptation for some directors under pressure, knowing that once a particular programme had finished recording that X or Y actor would ostensibly be free for casting in their own upcoming production when the bother of their scouring agents' lists and casting directories could be bypassed.

Yet again, in the late 1970s there was interchange of traffic between directors scheduled to work on Doctor Who and the new sci-fi series 'Blake's Seven'. As I had been under contract on Doctor Who for a while I was possibly considered as being 'in the building' – so maybe that is why my name came up as being free, both in 1978 and subsequently the following year to be cast in two separate 'Blake's Seven' stories – first as 'Pasco', a crew member of a Galaxy class space cruiser on a 'Mission to Destiny', and second as an outrageously louche character in a story called 'Gambit'.

'Mission to Destiny' was basically a 'whodunnit' in space, when a murder in a sabotaged space cruiser is uncovered, but 'Gambit' was something else entirely -

'as camp as a row of tents' - as the saying goes. The storyline was reasonably bizarre in itself, and there was a heavily implied suggestion of a gay relationship between my own character 'Toise' and that of Aubrey Woods as 'Krantor'.

Once 'Gambit' had been broadcast there was outrage within the top echelons of the BBC hierarchy together with a flood of internal memos of disapproval: heavens! Anything remotely 'gay' should have been consigned for viewing well beyond the 'watershed' of nine o'clock. This was 1979, remember. Both Aubrey and I were dressed like dandies from the French Second Empire: Aubrey himself a vision in a silver costume with a powdered wig and a beauty spot, my own elaborate rig being topped off with something like a chandelier as a head-dress which threatened imminently to fall off my somewhat loose-fitting wig! It was certainly a sea-change from playing K9 ... besides, I had the added bonus of renewing acquaintance with Jacqueline Pearce whose work I had greatly admired but who I hadn't seen since our RADA days together. As 'Servalan' she was imperiously sexy as the Supreme Commander of the Terran Federation.

ONWARDS AND UPWARDS

Back again in the outside world, 1979 had been a busy year for me. It had included a theatre season at The Brewhouse Theatre in Taunton and a guest appearance on a popular BBC television sitcom starring Martin Jarvis and Diane Keen. At that time 'Rings on Their Fingers' was one of the BBC's 'top ten' rated programmes, featuring its two stars as a bright young couple riding the roller-coaster of engaged and married life. It eventually attracted audiences of over 20 million.

The same 'post-Doctor Who' year also found me with my first role in a feature film for cinema: 'Tarka the Otter'.

No, I know what you're thinking – another animal part! Rest assured I wasn't cast as the hero of the piece no matter how many furry costumes I have worn in my past. My agent had put me forward to play the part of the Secretary to the Otter Hunt, and I was called to meet David Cobham, a writer, producer and director whose track record of producing nature programmes for the BBC was second to none.

My agent was delighted when a call came back from David's office confirming that I'd got the part. He was just a little cautious, though, and called the office back.

'You do realise, of course that you've cast John as a huntsman?'

'Yes, that's right'.

'I did tell you when we first spoke, didn't I, that John doesn't ride'.

There was the discernable sound of hearty laughter at the other end of the phone.

'You can tell him you don't ride to otters!'

'Tarka', based on Henry Williamson's 1928 novel, was filmed in period costume where the story is set, a beautiful location around two rivers in Devon. I hadn't realised until starting on the film that the otter huntsmen of the day pursued their quarry by actually wading waist-deep in the water, accompanied by a pack of otter hounds. These rare creatures are quite unlike any other hounds I have ever seen – great shaggy sandy-coloured beasts as big as Alsatians. Hunting such enchanting and relatively rare creatures as otters seemed to me a complete anathema, and I was relieved to hear that the sport had been banned the year previously.

A substantial pack of otter hounds still existed in Northumberland, however, presumably with nothing to do but drag-hunt, and this was brought down especially for the film. We 'huntsmen' were dressed in open-weave blue tunics and breeches, and grey bowler hats, making us look possibly more suited as doormen to a Mayfair hotel!

The author of 'Tarka', Henry Williamson had been invited initially to write the film-script, but he was very ill at the time and declined, the task falling subsequently to the writer Gerald Durrell. Williamson's son was co-opted as one of the film extras, and gave advice where needed on his father's behalf.

From a 'props' point of view one might imagine that filmed views of open Devon countryside wouldn't have changed much since 1928 – but I recall that local dairy farmers had to move their black-and-white

Holstein/Friesian herds out of fields that were designated to be in camera-shot and replace them with loaned Red Devon cattle, as in 1928 Friesians had not yet been introduced to the UK.

We noticed an interesting phenomenon: as time went by the lunchtime catering wagon seemed to attract an ever longer line of diners.

Filming proceeded apace, and we realised that that word must have had spread amongst the vagrant and travelling community living thereabouts: roughly-dressed themselves, they were tagging-on to the back of the queue of period-dressed extras, collecting themselves a free meal!

There was an ironically tragic finale to our filming, however. On the morning of the very last day of shooting which would involve Tarka's death-tussle with the otter- hound 'Deadlock', the pack of twenty hounds was being shepherded by its handlers into a specially adapted caged vehicle. During this process one of the hounds must have caught the scent of a mink, common vermin in the locality. He was off, with the rest of the pack following after him, breaking away across the fields, baying loudly and disappearing into the distance. Obviously no more filming could happen involving them until they'd all been rounded up. However, the dreadful news soon filtered back to us that the majority of the pack had run down some hangings and across a railway line at the very same time a train happened to be passing. Two of the hounds had been killed outright - other injured ones having subsequently to be destroyed. This was shocking enough of itself, but on the radio news at lunchtime that very day confirmation came through that Henry Williamson, author of 'Tarka the Otter', had died, just as our own 'Tarka', a tame otter called 'Spade' was being filmed in his fatal final scene. The further irony was that we needed an otter hound to play 'dead' after his cinematic underwater tussle with Tarka, and a local vet had already volunteered an elderly Alsatian that was going to have to be put down anyway. This dead dog had been brought to the location that morning with great ceremony, to be worked on by make-up artist Elaine Smith to make it look as much like an otter hound as possible. We little suspected at the end of that fateful filming day that we would have been able to provide at least three genuine dead otter hounds of our own.

My only other appearances on the cinema screen since that time have been cameo performances: I can be seen as a television interviewer quizzing Peter Cook in 'Whoops, Apocalypse!', directed by Tom Bussman . On that occasion, and to my great delight, I did get to meet Loretta Swit ('Hot Lips' Houlihan from MASH). Coming right up to date I can be seen as the shabby owner of a hardware shop 'somewhere on the Yorkshire moors' in Ian Vernon's prizewinning black comedy 'Rebels Without a Clue'.

* * *

K9 RENAISSANCE

Towards the end of my action-packed 1979 I was somewhat surprised to receive a further phone call from the Doctor Who establishment. John Nathan-Turner was a new name to me. He introduced himself and told me that he had taken over as producer of Doctor Who and wondered if I could help him with a problem.

'David Brierley has told us that he doesn't want to continue as K9 – and we wondered if you'd like to come back.'

Reacting to my stunned silence he said 'We're running K9 out of the series across the next few stories, and we'd like to see him go properly – is there a chance you could consider playing him again?'

Standing by the phone the words of an old school motto *Nulla Vestigia Retrorsum* suddenly came into my head – i.e. 'I am never taking a backward footstep'.

Did I have a weak moment?

JN-T was sufficiently persuasive. For all its well known physical limitations I liked the soul of the character I had created. The rest, as they say, is history.

The 1981 season of Doctor Who included the stories The Leisure Hive, Meglos, Full Circle, State of Decay and Warrior's Gate, the last three stories comprising the E-Space trilogy, at the end of which K9 remains in E-Space with Romana 2 – Lalla Ward. Full Circle was notable in introducing the character of

Adric as a new companion, played by newcomer Matthew Waterhouse, who stayed with the series some way beyond my own departure. Matthew's detailed account of his time on Doctor Who can be read in his book 'Blue Box Boy'. Previously an employee of the BBC's news-room, his sudden elevation to prominence as a companion caused a certain amount of surprise and concern. I was somewhat sympathetic to his plight.

A fish out of water, he had been thrust summarily into the rôle with no previous acting experience, and I witnessed directors having to take him aside on occasion during studio recordings to give him detailed attention. I suspect this was as much to his own embarrassment as to the possible frustration of the principals, all too aware of the time constraints involved in getting the show 'in the can'.

By this time Lalla Ward and Tom Baker were an 'item', and I well remember Judy and I entertaining them both to dinner on one occasion when there was much playing 'footsie' between themselves under the dining table. Our son Guy, then aged about nine, had already been put to bed but he was aware that both Tom and Lalla were downstairs. Tom was very keen to meet him.

'Take me to see Guy' he boomed. 'I want to read him a bedtime story!'

Judy took him upstairs accordingly and Tom royally entertained Guy to what must have been one of the best bedtime stories of his life.

After Guy's return from school the following day Judy asked him whether he had told his friends about what had happened the previous evening.

'No' he said.

'Why ever not?' Judy asked. 'They think I'm silly. They think that I think my daddy is K9 and that Doctor Who comes to dinner.'

I am more than lucky still to be working on occasion with Lalla Ward, who is equally talented as a graphic artist and as a fine actor. Though she has now officially retired from 'the business' she allows herself to makes exceptional forays into the recording studios to reprise her rôle as Romana in audio CDs.

BANISHMENT

And so to the end of the story 'Warrior's Gate'.

E-Space is no place to find oneself off-loaded from Doctor Who – even when one is destined to stay at heel with Lalla as 'Mistress Romana'. It is far too cold at nights, for one thing. No. I jest. Suffice to say that there seemed to be no further place for K9 within the thrust of the storylines.

K9 was shunted into the ether. However...

I completely failed to realise what was going on in the undergrowth in the outside world of fandom. Apparently there had been a groundswell of support for the K9 character, with bitter complaints to the BBC and to the media that he had been consigned to the sidelines, and it was therefore decided that there might be some further mileage in a spin-off series 'K9 and Company', which would also see the return of former companion Lis Sladen in a rôle as journalist 'Sarah-Jane Smith'.

The pilot episode for what was hoped would be a fully-fledged series was made by BBC Birmingham, with filming in the local countryside around.

The somewhat gothic storyline involving a coven of witches and the threatened human sacrifice of Sarah-Jane's young ward Brendan had been written by Terence Dudley. The cast included veteran actor Bill Frazer, and the programme was eventually broadcast as a Christmas 'special' that year. True to the form of my mainstream work in Doctor Who I also went to the locations, though I added K9's film dialogue at the post-production stage. It was there that I witnessed a rather chilly scene one night when a band of swathed female 'background artistes' (formerly known as 'extras') circled around their human sacrifice invoking the goddess of witchcraft, chanting

'Hecaté, Hecaté, Hecaté, Hecaté...' in a rhythmic fashion. Due possibly to the lateness of the hour and the likelihood of overtime payments, some had already started to chant

'Equity, Equity, Equity, Equity...' instead.

Sadly the story, 'A girl's Best Friend', remained a one-off partly due to budgetary constraints and partly, as I understand, due to a 'new broom' in the higher echelons of the BBC deciding that every dog has its day, and now it was K9's turn to quit the stage. I am not entirely sure how 'K9 and Company' would have been developed had it been given its head. Given that Lis Sladen's character was mortal, all the stories would have needed to be 'earthbound' rather than 'off the wall' and fantastical in the Doctor Who mode – but then one could argue that there were strong storylines in Lis's later model The Sarah-Jane Adventures which earned her series a substantial rating and viewership.

As history relates, Doctor Who was taken off the air in 1989, and I certainly didn't anticipate either its return, or the occasion of returning once more as K9. You may remember the following variant on the 'light-bulb' theme:

How many Doctor Who fans does it take to change a light bulb?

None. They all stand round the light bulb, hoping, willing and praying that it will come on again, and – amazingly – after nearly sixteen years it does! All by itself!

With the return of Doctor Who in 2005, with Christopher Eccleston's Time Lord having survived the Time War at some point in the interim – (forgive me, my grasp of Who-history has never aspired to accuracy) – there was not only a new Doctor and new companions but a completely new look!

Whereas the classic series had had to rely on a considerably less sophisticated technology, state-of-the-art digital computer graphics were now being pressed heavily into service enabling visual effects to be that much more spectacular and inventive than before.

Equally, writers were freed from any constraints the earlier sets might have imposed and could develop fast-moving plotlines that seemingly had no boundaries.

Though I always had a soft spot for 'analogue' Doctor Who and the 'real' monsters and creaky sets of the classic days I was impressed by what I saw, even though much of it was 'virtually' achieved.

Beyond that I was impressed by the fine balance that its guiding spirit, Russell T. Davies, had struck in keeping the classic Who-fans sufficiently on board while attracting today's audience of younger viewers, more greatly used to the vibrancy and speed of computer games in which things zip along on-screen. Could 'analogue' K9 survive in such an environment? I was far from sure.

I put all thoughts of ever playing K9 again out of my head and dismissed any rumours I heard at fan gatherings that he might possibly return.

Imagine my surprise when, in 2006, wearing my other 'hat' as a local magistrate (q.v.) I was congratulated by colleagues at my local court-house on my successful return to the series! This was certainly news to me, but apparently it wasn't to 'The Sun' newspaper. I was shown the page where it announced my triumphant return. Apparently, said 'The Sun', I was very happy about coming back again and had already signed a contract!

What it is to have 'The Sun' running your life for you, I thought.

Having heard absolutely nothing from the BBC about any proposed return, I thought this surprise public revelation might be my cue to call the Doctor Who office – now in Wales.

Given the distance of more than sixteen years since I last had any direct involvement with Doctor Who the response from the BBC was cautious, to say the least. 'How do we know you are John Leeson?' they asked, supposing that I might be another 'plant' by the press. I offered my credentials as best as I could, but the best they could finally offer me was worthy of 'Yes, Minister' – 'we can neither confirm nor deny that K9 is coming back'.

Frustrating, of course, but still not confirmation I could rely on. I recalled the fact years previously of having once received a letter from the BBC addressed to 'the Estate of the late John Leeson'. A mistake, as it turned out. My agent at the time was furious. I rang the BBC who duly apologised and told me that an accidental computer keystroke had been made, thereby causing the error. Actors' lives hanging on a BBC computer keystroke! What a thought.

The following week the position was resolved – an official call came through inviting me back to reprise K9 in 'School Reunion'. Perhaps, with hindsight, I should have taken the precaution in return of saying 'how do I know you are the BBC?', but in the event it proved not to be necessary.

I was delighted to hear that the story would star not only the new Doctor, David Tennant, but the lovely Lis Sladen who would reprise Sarah-Jane.

I telephoned Lis to tell her the news and she, looking forward to seeing me again, told me her own recording dates, hoping that once I knew them they would mesh with hers.

Time passed, and again there was an ominous silence from the BBC. Lis's filming dates had now come and gone, and I was getting just a little concerned that unless I had sufficient notice I might not be able to tie-in with her recording schedule in the studio.

Weeks passed, and eventually a call came through from Executive Producer Julie Gardner to say that 'School Reunion' had now been wrapped up, and could they book me next week to go into a dubbing theatre in Soho to lay on the voice-track for K9. I had mistakenly anticipated being used 'live' during the studio recordings as in the old days, but obviously a progressive new system prevailed.

It certainly saved the BBC paying travel expenses and an overnight fee for me in Cardiff, but the fact that no 'live' input was required from me meant the inevitable loss of the interactive dynamic that had helped the dialogue bounce between K9, the Doctor and others, in earlier times. Although K9 is seen to be acting with The Doctor in the story, I only got to meet David Tennant (an enthusiastic K9 fan) at a much later stage at a gathering in London.

Lovely Lis Sladen was certainly then, and later in her own series 'The Sarah-Jane Adventures', 'K9s Best Friend'. Although for technical reasons I hadn't been able to join her to work on 'School Reunion', watching it on transmission I thought she looked wonderful — she had hardly aged across the years.

Bearing all this in mind and coming much more up to date, I was deeply shocked and saddened immediately on my return from conventions in Australia and New Zealand to hear from Ian Levene that Lis had just died.

Unbelievable.

A fact confirmed shortly after his call on that evening's BBC News.

I could imagine, too, the devastating shock suffered by her husband Brian and her daughter Sadie, let alone to her devoted fans worldwide.

K9 SERIES

The 1981 pilot 'K9 and Company' aside, there had been a great deal of whispering in the 'fan' undergrowth and elsewhere about the possibility of a discrete, non-BBC, 'rejuvenation' of a digital K9 in his own series. I admit that I had paid little attention to the rumours, assuming, somewhat grandly I suppose, that if it were to be made and that they still wanted my voice, someone would be in touch with me to sign me up. As I now learn, K9's creator Bob Baker and producer Paul Tams were to have produced a four-part pilot series to be called The Adventures of K9, but development proved problematic due to difficulties not only in securing the rights but also the all-important funding for it. In 2006, however, there was another attempt to get K9 back in circulation. Jetix Europe (later Disney XD) had secured a deal with Bob Baker, Paul Tams and a London-based distributing company, but this venture, too, was eventually shelved.

In 2007, however, there appears to have been another spurt of energy on K9's behalf, tying-in with his reappearance in the BBC's Doctor Who 'School Reunion' episode. The Australian Film Finance Corporation came up with some money! Disney XD and distributors Park Entertainment were now enabled to produce and pre-sell a twenty-six episode series (now called K9) to Australia's Network 10 ... to be filmed in Canberra (doubling for London) ... which would be given further licensed distribution thereafter. I had a call from Paul Tams giving me a brief outline of the tortured progress the new K9 series had been making to the screen, together with an invitation to return and voice his dialogue.

Apparently the Australians had been scratching their heads worrying about re-casting the K9 voice, and hadn't thought of going to the 'fountain head' himself. Paul had to make a push for them to consider my doing it. For me, digital technology being what it is these days, it meant a series of visits to sound studios in Soho rather than repeated trips to Canberra to lay on a voice track. Well in any case it is rather more carbon-friendly!

DOCTOR WHO CONVENTIONS

In 1977, at the time of my arrival in Doctor Who, the concept of fan conventions devoted to the series was almost unknown. Even though in those days Doctor Who was one of the most popular and iconic series on BBC Television, there was nothing like the groundswell of fandom that currently obtains. Equally, 'BBC Enterprises', the BBC's marketing arm at the time, hadn't properly woken up to the opportunity of obtaining extra revenue from licensing merchandise.

Who spin-off series like 'K9 and Company', 'Torchwood' and 'The Sarah-Jane Adventures' were still barely twinkles in the eyes of their creators. Today the fan-base covers the English-speaking world wherever the programme is shown, and whether commercially run or simply fan-generated, conventions are now a thriving part of the support framework for the series.

I have no memory of the first British Doctor Who convention I attended but I well remember my debut as a celebrity guest – the only celebrity guest – in Philadelphia in the USA where the series was aired on the PBS Network. I was flown to 'Philly expecting to find myself somewhere down the bill alongside a Doctor or two, or at least one of the more notable companions, and was astonished to be told on arrival that as the voice of K9 I alone was the 'star' of the weekend. No pressure, then!

On arrival at the convention hotel I was introduced to the man who had been deputed to be M.C. of the event who asked me how I would like to be introduced at the grand opening of the proceedings at 4.PM the following day.

Given that K9 was a voiceover character none of the fans really knew what John Leeson looked like. This, I felt, was a situation worth exploiting, added to which it could prove an opportunity for a bit of fun. I suggested to the M.C. that I should be let loose quite anonymously in the convention during the course of the day dressed as a fan, complete with Doctor Who scarf, badges and camera etc... and that I should attend the opening ceremony as a member of the audience as if awaiting my own arrival. The M.C. meanwhile should make an announcement from the stage to the effect that John Leeson has been delayed coming from the airport, and until he arrives he would host an impromptu 'K9 sound-alike' competition with the fans. I myself should be allowed to take part, albeit incognito... but at all costs I shouldn't be allowed to win.

To fillet a long story down the dorsal fin I found myself the runner-up in the competition, just as I'd planned. Having then been sent back to my seat in the audience the M.C. pretended to receive news that I'd just arrived at the hotel, giving me an heroic build-up. All the faces in the hall turned to watch my arrival through the double doors at the back of the hall, and all I had to do was simply to get up from my seat and go back on stage. Seldom if ever have I received such an ovation! My cover had now been 'blown' completely, of course, and it was not the kind of trick I could ever have repeated, but my goodness, if ever there was a way to make a notable entrance, that was it! I sometimes wonder quietly whatever happened to the little guy who actually won the contest.

I had attended the Philadelphia convention on the basis that my flight and hotel expenses would be fully covered, but instead of paying me a fee the organizer said she would fly me across to Beverley Hills after the event, when she would put me up at her expense for a week in the legendary Chateau Marmont Hotel on Sunset Boulevard! Handsome payment indeed, at her own suggestion, albeit payment I couldn't put in the bank.

The organizer treated me as her personal guest who deserved to be shown something of Hollywood. She herself was quite a character. Middle aged, she lived in Van Nuys and bred pit-bull terriers, a fact I found slightly alarming, not that I encountered any of them. (I had a distant childhood memory of having been bitten once by my grandfather's temperamental Staffordshire bull-terrier). Equally she seemed to want to show me the darker side of Los Angeles, and insisted we visit Forest Lawn, the huge memorial park and funeral home in nearby Glendale.

It wouldn't have been my own choice for a day's jolly outing as the place spoke volumes about the American Way of Death as immortalised (if that's the right word) by Evelyn Waugh. It turned out nonetheless to be fascinating in a somewhat ghastly way - a visit that certainly revealed some of the wilder excesses of West Coast mawkishness.

She also took me as her guest to the rambling Edwardian mansion 'The Magic Castle', the exclusive dining club in the Hollywood hills for magicians and magic enthusiasts, of which she was a member. I think she was secretly pleased to watch my genuine astonishment as a result of both visits.

Noisy plumbing aside – and I dare say it may have been cured now - the Chateau Marmont Hotel was a wonderful place for people-watching, and I half recognized one or two famous Hollywood faces en passant, but the only person who drew me into conversation there was a charming, smartly dressed and attractive Englishwoman in her thirties who, sitting in the lobby and having heard my own English accent, pumped me for information about myself.

I told her what had brought me to this place, when she excused herself and said she'd be back in an hour as she was just visiting a friend. Could I stick around? She very much wanted to talk some more. I had almost decided to do so when the penny dropped. Something was not quite right. A member of the hotel staff confirmed my instinctive curiosity. The lady was apparently a regular hotel visitor, especially by private appointment to gentlemen guests.

Top-class nonetheless – and I dare say very expensive into the bargain.

Some years later I was listed as a guest at the massive multi-stranded convention in Chicago which took in 'Star-Trek' and Marvel Comics among various other sci-fi platforms which were then in vogue including, of course, Doctor Who.

Because of the vast number of attendees at the convention hotel at LAX airport, and the high profile of some of the celebrities there was a strong emphasis on our personal security. One travelled nowhere in the hotel without an escort, something I found rather difficult to accept considering my own low profile as merely the 'voice' of a character. Apart from the pressure of the weekend's autograph signing and flesh-pressing I well remember escaping from my less than watchful minder to find myself being accosted in a lift, (sorry, an 'elevator') by a hyper-obese female fan attending the event. She had spotted me as I was retiring to the safety of my room on the eighteenth floor following a lengthy session of autograph scribbling. As the doors closed she waddled into the lift after me ... given her formidable size there was only just room for us both ... and announced that she knew who I was and how wonderful it was to see me.

She enquired if I was now going up to my room. Quite innocently I confirmed that I was, whereupon she whispered to me that she 'knew a lot of positions'. I am seldom lost for words, but with eighteen floors thinking time ahead of me and possibly in excess of eighteen stone (250+ pounds) of weight confronting me I tried to construct a response that embraced lack of amazement in my voice with a firm 'no thank you' while at the same time not wishing to crush her sense of self-esteem.

By the time the lift had reached the tenth floor my surprise had recovered sufficiently for me to mumble a reassuring 'I'm quite sure you do' in response before making my escape to the sanctuary of my room, she herself being too slow and cumbersome to catch up with my retreating passage.

On a later occasion I had an opportunity to revisit Phoenix, Arizona, as a celebrity convention guest. I remembered only a little of the Phoenix I had encountered on my previous 'Shakespearean' trip in 1964 as a student with RADA. On arrival I saw that what I had considered 'out-of-town' was now pretty much 'down-town', so much had the city expanded in the interim. This particular convention celebrated not only Doctor Who but the then recently-released film 'Blade-Runner'. Beyond the cell-cool air-conditioning of the hotel the outside temperature that weekend was unusually hot even by Arizona standards... around 115F/46 C in the shade!

The personal temperature gauge of some of the fans seemed to be equally inflamed: some were running wild around the hotel and grounds with live side-arms, reminding me forcefully that the word 'fan' derives directly from the word 'fanatic'. Any idle musing on semantics aside, it was confirmation to me that Amendment Two of the US Constitution was being well upheld!

* * *

Tan'gent: *(-j-). a. & n. 1. Meeting a line or surface at a point but not (when produced if necessary) intersecting it.* (OED)

As my own journey bears witness, an actor's career is seldom straightforward. A colleague of mine once likened it to the progress of a twig floating in a fast-flowing stream. There will be stretches along the bank where the stream rushes ahead unimpeded, bearing the twig forwards headlong until maybe it gets caught up somehow, either catching on overhanging branches or getting stuck behind some rocks, when its progress is temporarily stalled. After a while the force of the stream releases it again until it meets a further obstruction – a backwater, perhaps, where it appears to drift quietly awaiting showers of rain that will enable it to float its way back into the main stream. There is the alternative analogy, of course, particularly applicable in my own case. Just as motorways and main roads can get you to your final destination more quickly, side roads and byways frequently offer more interesting scenery, plus the time to notice it, except that one's goal is reached that much more slowly. My own offbeat career has certainly been blessed with plenty of 'scenery' which, if translated to 'experiences' can be stored away in the metaphorical memory banks, later to be utilised if required by the specific demands of any particular role .

My life has offered me brief experience of a wide variety of fascinating activities, some of them more profitable than others, but useful in their own way. I was once signed up to sell encyclopaedias in the East End of London.

This was not particularly fertile ground as it turned out, possibly because I was hopeless at embracing the 'hard sell' mentality of my little band of fellow salesmen. I know I got to see more men wearing string vests than I'd ever seen in my life before. I was told to target women pushing prams in the street in the afternoons, when I'd make an appointment to visit them later in the evening when the man of the house could take an interest too. The 'button' I was instructed to push was the future education of their child. They'd want their kids to have an advantage, surely, over those that didn't have the material that I was offering them. I lasted a week in the job, not having sold a single copy.

In complete contrast I had experience in an independent London fashion house as a 'catwalk commentator', describing in flowery terms to the gathered audience at the occasional fashion shows the materials and the styles of the dresses being worn. Franka, whose maison it was, hailed originally from former Jugoslavia and excelled as a cutter.

A true heroine of the box pleat.

I even found temporary work in the West End of London as a waiter in a 'bistro' café where the owners, two large and rather tweedy ladies of a certain age spent the evenings sniping at each other. Both they and their clientele provided plenty of opportunities for people-watching, so the experience, though demanding in itself, was quite fun.

Outside my experience, thankfully, is wife-beating! I mention this only because I was once cast in an episode of the cop-show 'The Bill' as 'Mr.Witchell', a very inoffensive looking father who is 'shopped' by his schoolboy son for domestic violence against his mother. On my subsequent arrest I go berserk and even manage to assault PC Reg Hollis (Actor Jeff Stewart) – when my character's concealed violent attitude becomes patent for all to see.

Given the nature of my character's crime I remember thinking at the time that one never knows what goes on behind the privacy of other people's front doors.

MASTERMIND

Back in the 1980s, at a time of my own mixed employment prospects, Cherry Cole, a friend of ours and one of Judy's colleagues at the BBC, invited me to submit general knowledge questions for the 'Mastermind' series. I have never been a paragon of intellectual athleticism myself so the invitation came as an utter surprise. Cherry was a production assistant on the programme at the time and told me that one of the regular question setters was about to take a sabbatical.

'You've got a lot of bric-a-brac knocking about in your mental attic' she said, 'would you like to take the opportunity of using it? We need a freelance question-setter, and if you're interested I'll pass your name across to our producer, Bill Wright'.

What an irony, I thought.

Had I myself been sitting in the infamous black chair, a target of the relentless questions, I know my brain would have frozen stiff in an instant. However, Cherry encouraged me to submit a few questions on a try-out basis, and before long an official invitation came back for me to set yet more....each researched question attracting a tiny fee! I must have set a couple of thousand questions overall, each of which required three cast-iron references, as per my brief. 'Mastermind' is a particularly hungry beast when it comes to questions, and a fair proportion of them were reserved for use on the contestants' audition rounds, which the public doesn't get to see. The trick for the question-setter is obviously to set questions that can be answered in a word, the well-known time-pressures being what they are; the secret of success for the brainy contestant being his or her virtually instant recall, and a suitably snappy one-word answer in response.

Setting general knowledge questions was much less risky than setting specialist ones as in some cases the latter could attract different schools of thought - and the programme strove to avoid any contentious issues that might have caused difficulties with the contestants. Needless to say, perhaps, I learned a few arcane facts during my researches: you knew, for example, that there were such things as 'Fishes Royal'? No? Apparently 'whales, dolphins and sturgeons landed in the territorial waters of the British Isles automatically become the property of the Sovereign'.

All questions relating thereto should be directed to the Ministry of Transport. On a 'need to know' basis this is obviously useful stuff.

CELLE

Another offbeat byway I travelled, albeit on a short-term contract, was as a direct result of my freelance work in BBC presentation. BFBS, (The British Forces Broadcasting Service) was about to set up a small television station near what was then the border with East Germany for BAOR (British Army on the Rhine). The BBC had seconded one of their senior presenters, Colin Ward-Lewis, to head a dedicated team including a few BFBS radio presenters to get the service under way. Although a freelancer myself and not a member of BBC staff, I was asked if I would like to join them on a brief attachment, which I duly did. I was summoned to be vetted by BFBS and found not to be a subversive, and as I was to join a military establishment in Celle I was required to sign the Official Secrets Act.

Maybe under that particular constraint I cannot tell you anything about the military side of my brief engagement, but the television side is probably not difficult to guess at anyway bearing in mind what I have already detailed about my broadcasting work in

Manchester. At least I can describe some uncontentious generalities.

I found Celle itself a spick-and-span little town. Situated near the Lüneberg heath, it was almost a model for John le Carré's 'Small Town in Germany'. Proverbially, one could have eaten one's dinner off the streets they were so clean, and the little parish church which sat in the middle of the town like a mother hen watching over her chicks had a unique tradition of a trumpet fanfare being sounded at dawn to all quarters of the compass from the top of its lofty tower. A lasting legacy in thanksgiving, the village having been spared the ravages of the Black Death in the Middle Ages. I remember passing the church on my way to an early shift on a foggy autumn morning when the top of the church tower was completely invisible in the mist. The muffled sounds of trumpeting came seemingly from heaven!

For all the beauty and orderliness of the little town I remember the distinct frissons I felt both in discovering that the local bookshop still promoted copies and recordings of Hitler's speeches, and also in seeing the smart little yellow buses running round the town, some of which bore the destination board 'Bergen-Belsen' - the name of one of the neighbouring villages.

I learned something at first hand about the German sense of humour too. We had been showing 'Dad's Army' as part of our programme mix, and the three very charming local girls seconded from Radio

Bremen who ran the videotape machines were absolutely outraged by it.

'These are old men! What for is this funny? Why do you laugh at them so?' I tried to explain, but they'd have none of it.

'Nein! Es ist nicht komedisch, nicht wahr?'

I'd have to say, though, that the sight-gags of the euro-comedy 'It's a Knock-Out' had them in fits of helpless laughter every time we showed it.

BEADLE

My 'second career' in presentation also led me to a series of engagements that called for my core acting skills. The husband of one of the Presentation Editors at the BBC happened to be Head of Light Entertainment at London Weekend Television. Alan Boyd sounded me out for an assignment as a stooge on a new programme strand called 'Game for a Laugh' that had taken the famous 'Candid Camera' series as its matrix. I confess that I was just a little wary, as my required impromptu interactions with members of the public would have to be unrehearsed and improvised live on camera. I recalled how self-aware I had been back in my drama-school days when improvisation classes found us stretching our imaginations to breaking point. I had come a long way since then, of course, and yes, this job offer smacked of a challenge.

You may be aware of the premise of the series: unsuspecting members of the public are set up either by their family or by work colleagues to be spectacularly duped on television. My task was to join a little band of seemingly innocuous *agents provocateurs* who would lead them unwittingly into an artificial situation where their embarrassment in public would be the inevitable result.

From my own point of view, once the victim had been taken the first single step 'down the garden path' the subsequent ones were much easier to achieve. My job would then be simply to fade into the background, when prankster Jeremy Beadle, the show's host, would appear in disguise and then reveal to the 'punter' that everything had been a scam.

Laughs, tears, amazement all round ... or so it was hoped ... with the reward to the unfortunate victims of a live appearance in the studio when the filmed scenes would be aired. They, and not Jeremy, were the 'star' of the show.

Needless to say it was a format that required meticulous pre-planning and covert camera set-ups, and the 'punters' family or friends who had set them up in the first place were sworn to secrecy beforehand. This elaborate preparation – let alone the anticipation – seemed to me almost worthy of MI5 or secret police observations where the risk was present that our cover might be broken at any time.

I was usually cast as a 'jobs-worth' – a pedantic official who brooked no gainsaying. My sole aim was generally to convince the 'punter' that he or she was in the wrong and that I was in the right.

I quickly learned, too, just how gullible the British public can be in general, let alone how compliant in the face of instructions from bogus officials, especially ones wearing uniform of any kind.

On my first assignment I was 'the man from the bus company' tasked to get a lady to sign for a large bus shelter that had just been placed in her garden. In this case there had been an aggravating history of buses stopping unofficially by a rusty flagpole at the bottom of her garden, allowing passengers to alight there. To the lady concerned it had been a 'ruddy nuisance', and a running sore. What better than for her husband and daughter secretly to set her up to have an 'official' bus shelter on her own property? On the filming day her daughter had taken her mum shopping, having planted a hidden microphone in her handbag. Mum's first sight on arriving back at home was of a huge JCB vehicle lowering a bus shelter onto the back garden.

Mum's expostulations from within the car had to be 'bleeped' out to save audience blushes! She rushes indoors to fetch her (complicit) husband who, surprisingly, seems quite unfazed by the situation - she cannot understand his accepting attitude and drags him out to the garden to see.

To cut matters short, and to rub salt into the lady's wounds, 'the man from the bus company' now comes down the road. He is surprised that she is so irate. He tries to reassure her that there is absolutely no mistake. He confirms her address with her and assures her that the bus shelter is designated solely for her own garden. He stresses all its virtues – the chief of which are indestructibility and permanence.

You can imagine the kind of invective I myself am receiving at this point. The bus man's next strategy is to offer profuse apology: due to 'red tape' at the bus company she should have had this shelter at least six months ago ... she wouldn't want passengers to stand in the wet if it was raining, etc., etc.

I cannot imagine why the poor lady didn't physically assault me there and then. I anticipated scorch marks on my shirt, she was so incandescent with rage.

Enter Jeremy Beadle (thankfully) at this point – but although the lady had seen and enjoyed his programme on one or two occasions she was now wound-up to such a pitch that she completely failed to recognize him! It took many cups of tea indoors, tears, laughter, and general solace before our 'punter' finally came down to earth once again and accepted that she had been well and truly 'had'.

Reading all this you might wonder at the heartlessness involved in leading the innocent astray so publicly, but then the very essence of humour frequently contains a hidden seed of cruelty. The almost universal outcome of such scams is that the victim is only too willing to sign the TV company's release form, effectively enabling their own brief moment of stardom as a 'good sport' on this game show. For the wider audience there was half an hour of unmissable schädenfreude each week, so the show's popularity was assured.

One of the most inventive stunts that I remember was the engineering of a switch of vehicles aboard a tightly-packed cross-channel ferry. In this case the innocent victim was taking his family on a day trip to France. On arrival at the ferry he had been directed to drive to a particular slot on one of the ship's two parking decks where secret cameras had been set up. A low-loader truck concealing an almost identical car to his own had been parked strategically alongside. The elaborate car switch was made during the actual crossing of the Channel when the public is not generally admitted on the car decks, and filmed to be shown later before a studio audience in the presence of the victim.

On arrival in France the 'punter' and his complicit family naturally went to the car deck to pick up their vehicle only to find that it wasn't there! At least there was a car was in their place confusingly resembling theirs, but no, another driver came along to claim it and drive it away. The ship's parking bay was now totally empty.

The ship's embarkation officer was called for (in the person of myself) who tried to be as helpful as he could. As the shipping line we used was Scandinavian I decided I had to be 'Norwegian'. I could only express disbelief to the poor victim.

'I'm sorry, but you can see how it is. It is just impossible to lose cars on a tightly-packed parking deck during a crossing. Did you park it in the middle somewhere? Not at the side? Are you sure you've really looked for it?'

By this time our 'punter' was troubled beyond belief, so I asked solicitously whether he might not have made a mistake and not have brought the family car with him that day. Obviously my suggestion was ridiculed so I thought I should try and punch another button. 'How can this be our fault? That's ridiculous. Have you read the terms of our contract? We can take no responsibility for personal losses on board this ship – the notice over there sets out our liability in full'. The poor punter, now thoroughly balked and bamboozled, retired defeated to the upper deck with his family, to be accosted by Jeremy Beadle who 'revealed' the scam, showed the footage of the ingenious vehicle switch, and duly restored the missing car to its now massively relieved rightful owner.

Looking back, I think both I and my fellow scammers must have worked severally across three series of the show altogether. Although we were kept at the lowest possible profile on-screen lest we be recognized there was the increasing risk that we might be identified by an increasingly suspicious telly-watching public as the series progressed.

Apparently I need not have worried. At the time a further series was being mooted I accidentally met the executive producer in the street. He hailed me enthusiastically and asked me if I'd yet made up my mind to sign for the following series. I told him my reservations, but he waved them away airily.

'Of course you should sign, John' he said. 'You certainly shouldn't worry about being identified. In fact the wonderful thing about you John is that you are so f***ing unrecognizable'.

Just what an actor really wants to hear?

Taking what he said in the spirit in which I hoped it was meant, i.e. as a back-handed compliment, I assured him I'd think about it.

I seem to remember I signed.

Working with Jeremy Beadle put me alongside one of the most intelligent and widely-read entertainers then in the industry.

His business acumen had garnered a whole host of copyrighted game show formats worldwide, ownership of which must have made him a wealthy man way beyond his television appearances.

His beautiful house in north London was capacious enough to include an entire library floor crammed with volumes on philosophy, psychology, and just about every other subject under the sun. Personally generous and charming, he relished the title the press had created for him on account of his series as 'the most hated man in Britain'.

He was very much the metaphorical captain of his own ship – and I count him as a significant loss to the entertainment industry.

Aged about three, practicing for "Masterchef".

Aged about six, with my brother. *"When this chick grows up, Peter, I could make you a 'coq au vin'."*

Angelic choirboy.

As 'Feste' in "Twelfth Night" at Bryanston c. 1957

With The Leicester Symphony Orchestra. Cymbals at the ready!

Returning from Arizona, with Anthony Ainley,
Jonathan Holt and a friend.

Programme cover: 'Shakespeare on the Desert' 1964

As 'Leander' in the Nottingham Playhouse tour of "That Scoundrel Scapin".

With David Cook as 'Bungle Bear' in Rainbow. *This is a rare picture of the original costume. Bungle was redesigned subsequently*

Still from a German commercial for Herrenheuser Pilsner.

With Michael Keating and Colin Baker. 'Confusion Convention'.

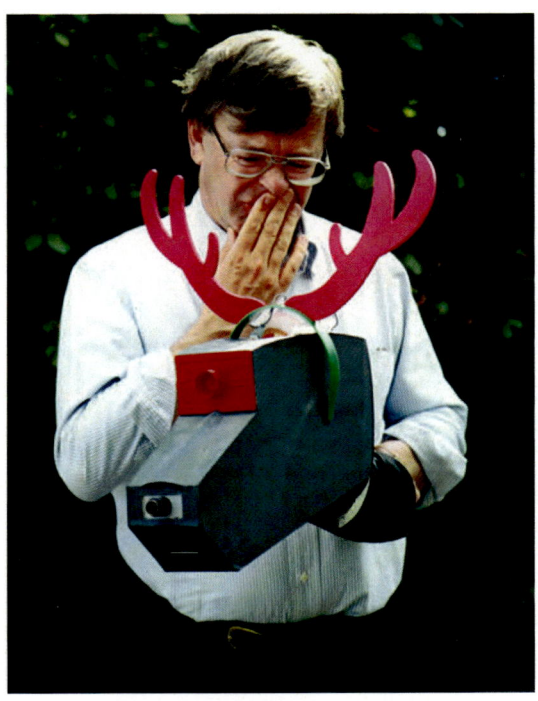

Mmmm… I think something's wrong.

'Shadow of the Noose'.   BBC 1989.

Taking K9 through his lines on location. 1977

Beatrix Lehmann.

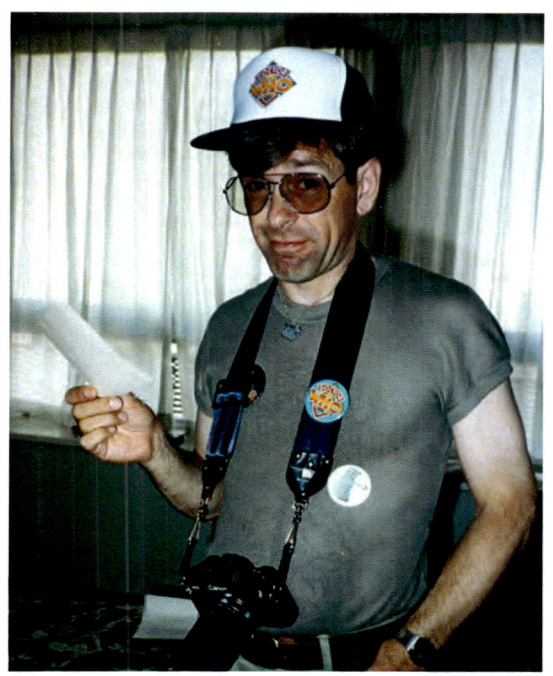

As a 'secret' Doctor Who fan in Philadelphia.

It's lonely being the only convention guest. Philadelphia.

Studio preparations – 'Cookin With Rita'. WHYY-TV

Cooking up a storm at home. 1980s-style.

Parade of K9's. 'Visions' convention, Chicago

As 'Mr Mulleady' in "The Hostage" with Geoffrey Beevers and Phillip Dunbar at Newcastle Playhouse.

As Sally Thomsett's hippy boyfriend in 'Comedy Playhouse'. BBC.

Rosemary Harris, myself, Gillian Lewis and Paul Rogers in "Plaza Suite" 1969. Photo credit: Reg Wilson

Downtime on a Lloyd's Bank commercial with Oskar Homolka.

With Michael Hordern in 'Flint'. 1970. Photo credit: Zoë Dominic.

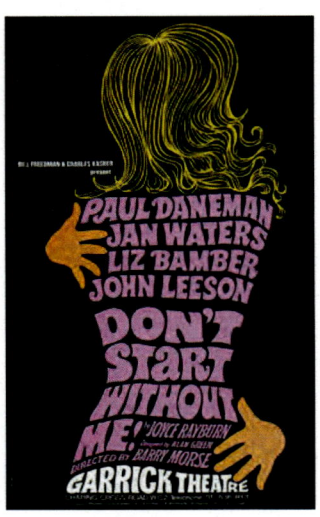

Poster for 'Don't Start Without Me'.

With Liz Bamber in "Don't Start Without Me, Garrick Theatre 1971.
Photo credit. Zoë Dominic.

From 1969's stage bridegroom to the real thing. With my wife Judy.

Chapter 4

*'Then the justice, in fair round belly with good capon
lined, with eyes severe and beard of formal cut'*
As You Like It

By the time you read this I dare say I shall have been required to retire from the active magistrates' bench by reason of age, not because my belly is not as round as it was, or for any surfeit of capon chickens in my diet. As a Justice of the Peace one is gently 'Transferred to the Supplemental List' at the age of seventy, when one's statutory powers are curtailed almost completely. A less harsh sentence, maybe, than being summarily kicked out as being too wrinkly to do the job properly. Ageism is still alive and well in the Magistracy, it appears, but as with most things I go uncomplainingly with the flow.

I was appointed as a Justice of the Peace in 1988 so I have had a good run – even being elected and subsequently re-elected in a run of successive years as Deputy Chairman of my bench.

K9 in a wig? (No, K9 ... magistrates don't wear wigs, just suits).

So how did all this come to pass? Were it not for the fact that the secretary of the wine club I joined years ago was herself a magistrate and knew that as an actor I occasionally had time on my hands, I dare say I would never have acceded to her suggestion that I should apply to join the magistracy.

Initially I turned down her idea as ridiculous. The 'powers that be', I thought, would never welcome an actor — a rogue and a vagabond — into their midst, so why should I waste time applying? She persisted and, in short, I put in my application a year later, backed by her own support.

By that time I had already taken the opportunity of visiting herown court to watch proceedings there. I admit I found them fascinating, not because the court itself had overtones as formalised theatre, but that the job of the bench appeared to be that of metaphorically sifting a multiplicity of shades of grey and defining them either as a black or white. An exercise in 'problem solving' in a fair minded and pragmatic way as case succeeded case.

The mills of the law grind slowly. I certainly didn't expect any positive outcome from the interview I was eventually summoned to attend.

This long awaited event proved to be a cathartic occasion. I was put under the microscope and dissected to the 'n'th degree by the appointments board before which I sat, and I well remember the relief and liberation I felt once the ordeal was over. I would never have to tangle with the Magistracy again, I thought, unless I had to be hauled up before the courts either as a witness or, worse, as a defendant.

Time passed. A further six months elapsed before I heard anything further, by which time I had long abandoned the cause as a non-starter.

Then, astonishingly, I received an important-looking envelope from the Lord Chancellor's Department containing a formal letter of acceptance. The word 'surprised' simply doesn't cover what I felt.

Mid-way through my career as a magistrate I found myself sitting alongside actor/playwright Anthony Marriott JP who had been transferred to my bench. I mentioned to him casually that some years previously I had been interviewed by him with a view to my taking over in the West End from Michael Crawford in 'No Sex, Please. We're British' – the record-breaking comedy he had co-written with Alistair Foot. He remembered my audition in some detail, and we both agreed that it had been no disgrace for me to have been pipped at the post for the part by actor David Jason. Anthony was still full of ideas for plays, and suggested that as we both had plenty of inside knowledge about the bench it would be great fun for us to write a comedy together about magistrates. We duly wrote 'Under the Bench', and then progressed over a couple of years to write a number of plays and television scripts together. At the time we wrote them they may well have excited ourselves and Anthony's literary agent but all our efforts have remained firmly and frustratingly on the proverbial shelf, gathering dust to this day. 'Under the Bench' actually received a private performance, though, as a fully cast rehearsed reading to an appreciative audience of magistrates!

Just as an afterthought: co-writing a play is a fascinating exercise. Anthony calls it 'marriage without sex'.

Interestingly enough, having read through what we had written together, neither of us could remember our own individual contribution of lines. We had met somewhere in the middle, proof of a collaborative partnership of equals.

The ideal place to be.

THE FOOD BIT

Had she lived to this day my mother would probably have forgiven me were I to describe her as a dutiful clergy wife, busied not only with her augmented family but also on hand to play hostess to the frequent visitors to the house on parish business. She was also the provider to the household in the days of rationing that extended beyond the war. I inherited a love of cooking from her, albeit that my earliest memories of vicarage cuisine were necessarily on the simplest side. I have memories rather more of 'nursery food' than anything more elaborate. When I arrived on the scene rationing was at its height.

As a child I rendered myself a complete nuisance following my mother round her kitchen, poking my nose into everything she was doing. My earliest memories of food were probably unpacked from post-war food parcels from the USA, very welcome goodwill gifts to wartime Brits from, in our own case, a certain Mrs Stack from Idaho, whoever she might have been. Apart from the then-ubiquitous powdered egg we had something approaching real ones as well, of course, the rubbery ones preserved in the larder in a bucketful of isinglass alongside the meat-safe, and regarded as 'precious'. I remember as a child checking to see how high or low they rode in this slippery liquid as an indication of their freshness.

Whereas most children would have been content with the more conventional toys, and indeed I was not short of them, my mother used to find me most happily occupied playing with off-cuts of raw pastry from her baking.

This, to me, was far better than plasticine or the more modern equivalent, 'play-dough'. My earliest attempts as a patissier were totally inedible of course, the pastry having been rolled around the floor to see how much dust it could attract. But tiny hands had made a start.

My studied efforts are a matter of record: my mother's photograph of me aged about three, brow furrowed in concentration at the pastry-board, hangs above the worktop in my kitchen to this day even though sixty-plus years onwards I'm still no great shakes as a pastrycook.

At least my mother nurtured my own early adventurism in the kitchen: I remember she once entered me in a cake-making competition at Leicester's

Abbey Park Show where my childhood efforts with a Victoria sponge earned the 'Very Highly Commended' accolade.

Well, one has to start somewhere.

Later in my childhood I remember my mother told me the cautionary tale of our wartime family butcher who would sell on occasion a mysterious (and strangely un-rationed) meat he labelled as 'Roof Rabbit', not that it ever appeared across our threshold. My mother was pretty clued up whenever that alternative commodity found its way onto the butcher's hooks and steered well clear of it. Maybe our own family moggies at that time, Jasper and Janie, were lucky to have escaped being caught and skinned by our local version of 'Dad's Army's Corporal Jones the butcher. Jasper, though, had his own cavalier attitude to rationing. Had he not been a cat he might even have been brought before the courts for flouting the strict and necessary regulations of the time.

He had wandered one day into the kitchen of an adjacent school where he consumed the entire complement of rabbit livers that were about to be cooked for the children's lunch. There was uproar, and he was carried home in ignominy, stiff as a board, being too bloated to move a whisker!

In the austerity days of the 1950s I remember powdered milk, which I liked, and I have a vivid recall of 'Ministry of Food' orange juice in small bottles, its fluorescent colour as concentrated as its flavour. Dandelion coffee is another substance that comes to mind, a caffeine-free substitute for the real thing. I am sure I wasn't offered it as a child, nonetheless I vividly remember the aroma whenever the tin was opened, its herbaceous, rather bitter scent pervading our kitchen when the room wasn't otherwise reeking with clinker fumes from the AGA solid-fuel cooker, freshly stoked with postwar-quality coke.

Looking at my own bookshelves and thinking back, I seem to have inherited my mother's passion for collecting and adapting recipes. In her own day my mother's household mentors were books and magazines from 'Good Housekeeping' and the cookery writings of Constance Spry, Ambrose Heath and Marguerite Patten, written at a time when British kitchens were moving only slowly away from scarcity. Substitute foods abounded, generally in powdered form, yet my inventive mother always seemed adept at creating something out of nothing that tasted vaguely 'real'. At this distance of time I have no wish to criticise her cooking, but for all her culinary ingenuity I must now confess many of her meals tasted really vague! Today, for example, well flavoured extra-virgin olive oil can be found in variety and without difficulty on the shelves of most supermarkets, however I remember that my mother had to make do with the little bottles of purified olive oil obtained from Boots the Chemist - a substance from which any vestige of taste seemed to have been surgically removed! There seemed to be no great general precedent at the time to opt for vibrant flavourings in food and my mother was naturally cautious in the use of spices and seasonings. I still recall the time when she dished up a kind of lamb ragout bathed in an insipid, neutral sauce in the subtlest shade of beige. I remember my sister asking her what, if anything, her bland creation was called.

'It's a curry, darling!' Lapses over roast chicken (a real luxury then) occurred from time to time, when my mother forgot that the bag of cellophane-wrapped giblets needed to be removed from the cavity of the bird before it was committed to the oven.

I used to badger my mother daily as a child for details of what she was preparing for us, and she was always fairly secretive about desserts: 'What's for pudding, mummy?' I would ask. The answer 'Wait and See Pudding' frequently came back, a motherly rebuke for my impatient curiosity.

From time to time, however, the response was,

'A shape, dear'!

Clearly yet another insipid blancmange was in preparation, masquerading either as a broody hen or as a rabbit on its haunches depending on which of the two moulds my mother used.

In later life my own kitchen mentor was food writer Elizabeth David, the unseen guiding spirit behind much of what I tried to bring to the table. My enthusiasm for cooking had fuelled a useful skill during my bachelor life, so I am afraid that once I was married I rather commandeered the kitchen at home. I am happy to be the regular household cook and, mercifully, my wife still seems very content with the prevailing position. I can imagine the unremitting pressure that working in a professional kitchen would involve, so 'cheffing' as a career was certainly not for me.

Our summer garden party here at home, (originally established to celebrate our son Guy's twenty-first birthday), has become something of an annual fixture and finds me catering single-handedly for around eighty people. Clearly I must slow down!

One of the convention attendees who had looked after me at my first *Who*-convention appearance in Philadelphia had discovered from whispers she had heard of me that I am a reasonably enthusiastic performer in the kitchen. She had contacts. On my arrival she asked me if I would like her to arrange my appearance as a guest on a local TV cook-show, 'Cookin' With Rita' on WHYY TV. I was flattered, naturally, but more than a little apprehensive. My original brief was to appear in the USA as a running character in Doctor Who and not as an impromptu television chef.

Cooking on camera was something I had never done before and I was aware of the tag that had been applied to me in my schooldays: 'fools rush in...' If nothing else, I thought to myself, it would be an experience, so I agreed to the assignment without too much further persuasion.

What on earth should I - could I cook?

I proposed cooking a couple of classic English dishes which would certainly be different to the kind of Philadelphia/Dutch cuisine that prevailed thereabouts – but had I thought things through sufficiently in advance? Could I get the basic ingredients I would require? Did I have access to the kind of kitchenware I needed for preparing my part of the show? As a result I found myself scrambling around the shops in an effort to get my metaphorical ducks in a row in time for the TV recording.

As it happened, Rita, whose show it was, was an experienced studio professional and a generous hostess to this foreign 'incomer', and my quintessentially English dishes appeared without mishap.

I am not sure how the studio audience of blue-rinsed Philadelphia ladies took either to this English stranger in their midst or to the dishes I prepared, but I learned subsequently that our recording went to air on July 4th that year, ironically on the anniversary of the day America celebrates getting rid of the English altogether.

Many years later my wife encouraged me to enter a Radio Times competition organized jointly by the BBC and Zanussi, the Italian kitchen appliance firm, to submit a recipe of my own that evoked 'the taste of Italy'. (Impossible perhaps if one knows something of the phenomenal diversity of Italian food across its twenty provinces!) I submitted 'my' variant of a dish I had tasted in Venice involving guinea-fowl. Thinking no more about it, and assuming the BBC would be swamped with competition entries, I was taken completely by surprise when about six months afterwards a letter arrived telling me that I'd won! The multi-part prize was arguably far more impressive than the dish I had created, comprising a long weekend for two at the exclusive Cipriani Hotel in Venice in company with top chef Antonio Carluccio who had judged the contest. In addition there was a seven-course Venetian 'winner's banquet' devised jointly by Carluccio and the Cipriani's chef. Finally Zanussi, the co-promoters, even offered icing on the proverbial cake: our choice of a free kitchen appliance!

While on the subject of 'food moments' across my career, I cannot help mention of a dish that takes me straight back to my time filming 'Tarka the Otter'. I wondered where the film crew had disappeared to one evening: clearly they had lighted upon a reasonable watering-hole. Judy had joined me on location, so the following evening we were directed to where it lay. Our journey down a winding single-track Devon road complete with grass growing down the middle of it brought us eventually to a tiny village which sported an ancient thatched pub. Film crews obviously have a 'nose' for good food. Our meal cost us as much as four pounds a head, and included three compulsory puddings even after one had tackled all one could manage of the complete napkin-wrapped Stilton cheese that was left at the table. Phenomenal value even in those days, particularly as the country-style cooking there was exemplary.

One of these 'compulsory' puddings, the delicious 'Duke of Cambridge Tart', is a well-nigh lost treasure of the English dessert board and has since found its way since into my extensive collection of favourite recipes. I share it with you at the end of the book.

So impressed had we been by this quiet oasis of comfort that Judy and I returned for a brief stay at the pub the following year, only to find that its owner and landlord had recently died. His wife Elizabeth (the cook) who was struggling to keep the show going knew we loved the place and asked us point-blank if we ourselves would consider taking it over. That night, lying in the pub's master bedroom (the one with the half-tester bed and the grand piano in it) Judy and I discussed the surprise invitation at some length, but wisely rejected it.

Though the offer had been extremely tempting at the time we realised nonetheless we would have been walking into a fools' paradise.

Our lack of management experience aside, to have run a country pub seemingly in the middle of nowhere would have meant an irrevocable sacrifice both of our established careers and our connections in London, let alone a completely new direction for our family life.

COOKIN' FOR LOOKIN': *my own expression for food appearing on film and TV whether consumed or not.*

Judy left work at the BBC in 1989 to become a freelance Production Buyer in the film and television industry, working alongside the art departments to provide props for a wide range of significant productions. (Her own autobiography, were she ever to write one, would put my own slim volume somewhat to shame!)

But to the point: there were just a few occasions when she would invite my own skills as a cook in providing on-screen food for the film she happened to be working on at the time.

I readily accepted her commission to provide a 'period' lunch party spread for 'Poirot' : 'The Case of the Missing Will' and somewhat later to prepare simple wartime food for a couple of episodes of 'Foyle's War'.

For 'Poirot' I had constructed an elaborate 'tower' of aspic jelly stuffed with quails and all manner of decorative savoury goodies. It had taken a good while to make, having been built up progressively as each layer of the jelly set. This was destined to be the grand centre-piece of the outdoor table display. Unmoulding this savoury edifice at the location gave me heart-stopping moments. With no replacement lest this one should collapse I realised I was taking a huge risk.

I consoled myself that I wasn't, after all, a professional home economist used to film requirements of several 'takes' when duplicate items had to be standing by in case they were required; in any event, the antique mould I had borrowed for the purpose was unique.

Mercifully my aspic 'tower' turned out perfectly and assumed its place at the centre of the table, surrounded by the other less demanding things I'd prepared for the occasion.

The day of filming was warm and sunny however, and while waiting for the previous scene to finish I saw to my horror that my jelly tower was threatening to become the leaning tower of Pisa. Would it collapse altogether before David Suchet and the rest of the cast started digging into it? Mercifully it didn't – just – but I had learned a salutary lesson.

Next time anyone wants to commission any on-screen jelly from me, I'll have to make it 'industrial strength'!

THE VERITAS OF VINO

It may seem odd that my childhood theft of sips from a bottle of dry Madeira on my father's sideboard should not have put me off wine for life. Even at this distance of time I can still recall what I then found to be a disgusting taste. I little expected some sixty years later that I would have developed a secondary profession as a wine educator and wine writer to complement my acting career. Wine was not unheard of when I was growing up at home, but it appeared only rarely at table. Having reached the legal age for alcohol consumption but seldom having the funds for it, I seem to remember that I generally dated girlfriends with bargain-basement Liebfraumilch, or the anonymous-tasting squeaky-clean Yugoslavian Riesling which then proliferated, to help oil the wheels of conversation.

Many years later, though, my serious interest in wine arose. This was possibly due to a magical bottle of Alsace Gewurtztraminer that Judy and I had shared in a restaurant in Paris.

Here, a kind of alchemy had been achieved: pure gold seemed to have been produced from the base metal of sap inside a vine stick.

To cut a far longer story short, both Judy and I promptly joined a wine club locally at home to enhance and widen our tasting experience. Years later, she funded my attendance at courses at the world-renowned Wine & Spirit Education Trust in the City of London in order for me to gain accreditation as a wine teacher. This was a particularly generous move on her part as by this time she herself had become allergic to alcohol in any form.

As a result I have been leading 'ad hoc' tastings, lecturing on cruises, writing and advising on wine ever since, as a member both of the Association of Wine Educators and (somewhat more recently) the Circle of Wine Writers. An auxiliary freelance career had been established, enhanced immeasurably by my continuing experience as an actor and presenter.

Sounds like a cushy job?

'To teach is to learn', they say, and one might be surprised how much research work is actually involved in setting up tastings, let alone the need to keep oneself up to date in an ever-expanding market by on-going training. Study trips to wine-growing areas also prove a valuable means of keeping oneself up to date with the latest technology.

If the idea of spending days tasting wines seems like a hedonist's heaven, then think again.

Judging wine at competitions is fearsomely exacting, and one's nose and palate can quickly tire.

I remember once being asked to join a group of colleagues conducting 'triage' tastings of 170 different wines from Portuguese growers seeking markets in the UK, the question being to determine their potential market acceptability to British-tuned wine palates. We tasted 90 wines in the morning and 80 in the afternoon, taking notes on every sample. Heavy on one's powers of concentration, it was one of the toughest days of wine-work I can remember.

Lecturing on cruises sounds a doddle in comparison, the disadvantage being that cruise lecturers aren't paid – however they do get to travel free of charge and they can usually take a guest with them as (fortunately) they have to be on board and 'on duty' wherever their ship sails!

I have been lucky enough to travel widely, as far afield as Muscat, the Seychelles and the Caribbean, though my usual 'beat' has been the Mediterranean. Perhaps the most 'educational' wine cruises, however, are those down to Cadiz in Spain as the ports of call can include not only Bordeaux but Spain's Rias Baixas wine area, Oporto in Portugal, and Cadiz itself, a stone's throw from the Sherry region.

It was on such a trip that I met a delightful lady who, seeing my badge as Guest Lecturer, confided that she herself belonged to 'something of a wine family'. I was politely interested and inquired whereabouts they made wine. 'Bordeaux', she said. 'The family is the Rothschilds'.

Although she was not 'into wine' herself, the very name found me knee-tremblingly in the presence of wine royalty. Apparently she was stopping off on the cruise to visit her cousin the Baroness Philippine at Château Mouton-Rothschild once the ship had docked in Bordeaux. For some unaccountable reason both she and her husband decided that I was worth taking with them on their visit to the family 'pad' in Pauillac, to be given a tasting there....and that was after their having treated me to lunch in Bordeaux at a Michelin-starred restaurant! Had I died and gone to heaven, I wondered.

Back on board ship the following morning my task of lecturing was somewhat compromised by a rough passage while crossing the Bay of Biscay. A far less glamorous experience than that of the previous day. The ship was pitching and tossing to the extent that one felt all the effects of excess wine consumption before one had even started, and most of my expected audience was absent, tucked up nauseously in their cabins, feeling too ill to move, wine tasting being the last thing on their minds.

THE HEART OF THE MATTER

I mentioned earlier that I had suffered damage to my heart a dozen years ago as a result of an infection picked up, so to speak, from the dance floor when I was auditioning for a commercial.

It is now time to reprise the subject: As a result of my having suffered endocarditis I spent several years thereafter in an un-rhythmic fashion, my heart firing metaphorically on only three cylinders rather than four. I had been told at the time of my earlier treatment that I would need to have a heart-valve repair operation at some future date, and such an event was planned to take place in October 2007. As a preparation for cardiac surgery I underwent a plethora of tests which, mercifully, included a full body CT scan.

I say mercifully because the scan revealed 'something' growing – quietly and painlessly - within my right kidney. Had it been left untreated it would have meant that this autobiography would probably have remained unwritten.

Judy herself had suffered and had mercifully recovered from a cancer not long previously, and obviously the matter of dealing with my own problem took immediate and urgent precedence over the needs of my waiting heart. Cardiac surgery was performed the following spring once I had recovered from the kidney removal operation. Thankfully one has two – that's kidneys, of course. I leave 'two hearts' to Time Lords.

I knew that having a heart operation was not something to be undertaken lightly, of course, besides, 'the heart' figures as far more than mere muscle, carrying resonances as the deepest seat of one's being and the centre of one's emotional life.

My surgeon, a man who specialized in the particular valve that was giving me problems, exuded confidence, so maybe there was nothing for me to fear but fear itself. Funny how things suddenly come to mind: I remembered an entry from Capt. Scott's diary at the end of his fateful expedition: '....we took risks, we knew we took them. Things have turned out against us therefore we have no cause for complaint'. He, at least, wrote bravely in the face of inevitable and anticipated disaster.

In my own case there was risk, certainly, but I was in good hands and, in the circumstances, trustful of a better outcome for myself.

It was perhaps a piece of good luck that on the morning of my operation the ward staff overlooked giving me any pre-medication.

Un-drugged, I felt something not unlike the sense of anticipation I get when about to go on stage – a heightened excitement and awareness. Mercifully I had never suffered from stage fright.

True, I was shortly going to appear in a 'theatre', and anyway I liked being well-lit ... so the show must go on.

The time eventually came for me to toddle along to the anaesthetics room where soft music was playing. My penchant for quickly identifying snippets of classical music hadn't deserted me. There, I recognized a movement from Haydn's Symphony No. 30 in C major... the so-called 'Alleluia' symphony.

Lying there being 'prepped', half smug at my powers of recognition and half amused, I wondered as I drifted away if the next 'alleluias' I would hear might be sounding for me on the other side! As matters have turned out the angelic trumpeters will have to wait a bit in their hope that I might yet turn up.

THE 'HILL OF BEANS'

Random thoughts bubble up on occasion, and I sometimes feel the need to catch the bubbles in print before they burst – so as I close I offer the following inconsequential thoughts as optional reading on your part.

Looking back at over forty-five years of my life in the profession I occasionally chide myself that I haven't been more single minded in keeping to its mainstream.

Having been born under the sign of Pisces – swimming in two opposite directions at the same time - it now looks suspiciously as if I have glided effortlessly through my career, accepting pretty much anything and everything that has come my way.

My achievements have certainly been off-beat in places. Have I purposely sought to hide away from the full glare of the limelight? How would I have made out had I travelled along the main roads to a supposed fame and fortune?

Open questions, I dare say, and so much has changed in the acting profession since I started out in it.

It is probably three times the size it was when I joined it back in the mid-1960s, and although the 'platforms' on which work is now available for actors have expanded in this digital age I dare say that job opportunities haven't increased to anything like the same extent.

It seems a particular pity to me that emerging actors nowadays have far fewer opportunities of learning their craft in front of live audiences.

Today the Repertory Theatre system as I knew it has all but disappeared. Arts subsidies have been cut back systematically across the years – and even as I write this there is serious debate among educationalists whether Shakespeare should still be taught in schools.

The economic climate is now such that wherever regional live theatre still exists it is now very much reduced in scale, and it seems more dependent than ever on 'names' from television to attract audiences. There was never any money in 'Rep'… but it was the springboard for so many well-recognized performers at the beginning of their careers: Dame Judi Dench, Lynn and Vanessa Redgrave, Patrick Stewart, Jeremy Brett, Dirk Bogarde and a host of others.

I can only pay tribute to the discipline the system provided in extending my own playing range in regular performances, let alone the opportunity it gave local theatre-goers to see a varied programme of plays on (usually) a fortnightly basis.

These days the professional casting directory 'Spotlight' puts out daily briefings which call as much for 'the genuine article' rather than for actors per se , no matter whether the performers who are subsequently cast are able to play anything wider than their immediate brief.

I stick my neck out, but I think professionalism in the arts is still under-valued. I make no criticism of amateurism, though, as its dynamic lies in an entirely separate direction. You may recall the inept 'pay-off' comment I received from the chairman of the theatre governors after my season at Dundee; and I have encountered other comments like 'does your boss mind you taking time off work to do this kind of thing?' I am told that the distinguished operatic bass Michael Langdon once found himself standing in a London underground train heading for Covent Garden at elbows-length from a neighbour of his whom he didn't know personally. The neighbour recognized him by sight and said

'I know we don't know each other, but my wife and I see you from time to time and we've wondered because of the odd hours you seem to keep what it is you do for a living. We've even argued about what we think you do. I wondered if you might be a burglar, always going out at night, but my wife is perfectly sure you must be a policeman'.

'No', said Michael, 'I'm an opera singer.'

'Oh well, ask a silly question…' said his neighbour, who then went into a huff and studiously ignored him for the rest of the journey.

It would seem to be borne out in my acting career that I am a useful team-player. I tend naturally to get on with people, and the only actors who really annoy me are those who make demands of attention at the expense of their professional colleagues and the time required to fulfil job in hand.

I have met more than a handful of vibrant personalities across the years who I might accuse of being overly self-regarding, but there are usually discernable personal reasons why they might feel the need to hog the limelight. As they said to us way back in our drama-school days 'there are no acting problems that are not personal problems', a fact I have seen and know to be true.

I can think offhand of only one well-known actor with whom I have worked who I have positively disliked on account of his own manifest self-importance, his rudeness and his chauvinistic behaviour towards his female colleagues, and he doesn't feature in this book.

Maybe I can think of one or two other prominent performers in whose company I might anticipate difficulty were I to work with them – but 'no names, no pack-drill'!

Although not meant necessarily in a pejorative sense, some hold the view that we actors are 'damaged goods'; perhaps 'incomplete' is a kinder word to describe us, our 'completeness' being manifest to ourselves once we are subsumed wholeheartedly into our roles.

Tom Baker speaks of actors 'celebrating' the characters they play, a perfect word to use. I applaud as much at the bravery of those actors in dramatic roles who take emotional journeys 'where angels fear to tread', as much I applaud the comedic skills of the 'entertainers' among us.

No matter how light or serious the intention of the scripts we are called upon to play, 'entertainment' is a base-line of what we are all about. Creative artistes aim to work from a truth to convey a truth – but even that is a slippery commodity.

Perhaps the well-known expression 'putting on a performance' is a paradox – in many cases one's performance as an actor is achieved less by 'putting on', i.e. adding layers, but rather more in discarding them to expose the 'centre', where the truth is supposed to lie.

A reductive process. When describing how to sculpt an elephant from a block of stone, Picasso advised 'simply cut away all the bits of the block that aren't elephant ... and there's the elephant'.

My random thoughts and views on anything, let alone on elephants, are all very well of course and may not amount to the proverbial 'hill of beans' at this chapter's heading. Though the principle is sound, I'll even hold my hand up if I'm wrong about Picasso! I can speak for myself, however, when I say that I have always found that the profession of an actor offers an exceptionally difficult circle to square: in the rehearsal process one needs to be virtually 'selfless', sensitive, and in a sense vulnerable, open to discovering where one's character and one's relationships sit; and on the other hand – simply in terms of advancing one's career – one has to be self-seeking, hard-nosed and competitive ... out there to prove oneself and win further work!

Employment prospects aside, it is no wonder that an actor's life is hard. Whether we are actors or otherwise it seems to me that our best way forward is to accept the security we have in our being insecure.

It is another paradox of course, but least it seems to help.

My life's journey started with a gentle ring of bells and, save for the janglings of my early youth it has continued as a manifestly mingled chime.

Where next, I wonder?

Oh, sorry, I have to stop! Another bell tells me I've left something in the oven!

-oOo-

THE RECIPES

Yes, I know - John's Autobiography: *Now with Recipes!* Maybe you'll consider it is an indulgence on my part to reproduce them here – but I take occasion to celebrate just one or two key food moments remembered across my career which, for me, have understandably become more than the sum of their original parts. Besides, you might like to share them anyway.

First, from Philadelphia and 'Cookin' with Rita':

APPLE AND BARLEY SOUP

INGREDIENTS (for 4)
1.5 litres of beef or chicken stock
500g Apples, (Bramleys or Cox Orange Pippin)
½ teasp. powdered ginger or good pinch of powdered saffron
black pepper to taste.
75 g pearl barley

METHOD
Pre-soak the barley in a little of the cold beef or chicken stock. Bring this to a very gentle simmering point and cook until the barley has softened. Reserve. Bring the remainder of the stock to the boil then add the peeled and cored apples, cut into chunks, and allow them to cook through until soft. Whizz in a blender or

(if you are being mediaeval) push the apple mush through a sieve. Combine all the ingredients, adding the ginger or saffron and the pepper, allow to cook together very gently for ten minutes for the flavours to infuse. Serve hot.

-oOo-

What follows is the prize-winning recipe I created for the BBC/Zanussi competition. Antonio Carluccio told me he didn't even have to cook it to appreciate its authenticity.

'The ingredients', he said, 'speak for themselves'.

GUINEAFOWL FRICASSÉE 'BURANO STYLE' (SERVES 4)

INGREDIENTS
1 Guineafowl (Cornish hen) cut up into convenient pieces
1 teasp. vinegar

The following ingredients finely chopped:
2 carrots,
1 stalk of celery,
1 clove garlic,
1 large onion,
4 or 5 green olives,
6 capers,

6 sage leaves,
1 tblsp. fresh rosemary,
1 Italian (or Toulouse) fresh pork sausage,
2 slices pancetta, or green bacon,
2 tblsps olive oil
5 fl.ozs. dry white wine
juice of half a lemon
a small strip of lemon zest
1 small tot of Grappa (or brandy)

METHOD - STAGE 1
Put the guineafowl pieces in a bowl of water acidulated with the vinegar and allow to steep for about half an hour. Chop all the other ingredients finely as directed, and mix them together in a separate bowl.

STAGE 2
Heat the oil in a fricassée pan. Pat the guineafowl sections dry with a paper towel and put them in the pan together with all the chopped ingredients. Let them take colour briefly then reduce the heat under the pan. Turn the ingredients from time to time and let them cook gently together until pale gold in colour.

STAGE 3
Add the white wine, the lemon juice, the strip of lemon zest and the Grappa, making sure the fluids are well mixed in. Cover the pan and allow to simmer on a very gentle heat until the guineafowl is tender.

WINE
I'd suggest a Gavi di Gavi DOCG from Piedmont, or a top quality Pinot Grigio from Friuli (Collio).

-oOo-

Finally, the indulgent dessert tart that I encountered while working on 'Tarka the Otter'. It is definitely not for the calorie-conscious!

DUKE OF CAMBRIDGE TART

INGREDIENTS: (PASTRY)
225g plain flour
100g fine ground almonds
150g butter
1 egg
100g caster sugar
½ teasp vanilla essence

FILLING
150g butter
150g caster sugar
6 egg yolks, beaten
2 -3 ozs candied peel
a few glacé cherries
a handful of muesli flakes (optional)

METHOD

Prepare a 8/9 inch pastry tin and line it with the pastry, having chilled it for half an hour or so.

Bake blind for about 12 minutes, remove the weights and allow tocool. Sprinkle the peel, cherries and muesli (if using) over the pastry case and set aside.

Over a medium low heat gradually bring the butter, sugar and egg yolks to boiling point in a saucepan. Watch out that the mixture doesn't burn, and beware spits from the pan.

Pour this mixture over the pastry case and its contents and cook in a slow oven (Gas mark 2) for about an hour and a half. NB: Timing is approximate, but the tart should be caramelised gently, not browned to a frazzle.

Serve hot, (or even better cold when there's a light toffee texture on the tongue!), with a dollop of chilled crème fraiche alongside.

-oOo-

The author and publisher would like to thank the following people:

Brian Adams
David Adler
Darren Allen
Tony Amis
Edward Allison
Andrew Barrett
Nicholas Blake
Philip Brennan
Adam Chamberlain
Darren Chandler
Alan Clyde
Mike Cook
Shane Cook
Steve Davies
Emma Elliott
Emma-Louise Elliott
Paul Engelberg
Scott Fraser
Ian Greenfield
Aaron Gregson
Rodney Hedrick
Tim Hicks
Mark Humphrey

Blayne Jensen
David Johnson
Chris Kerr
Derek Kettlety
Ceri Laing
Jim Lancaster
Christopher Leather
John Main
Kenneth Mason
Steve Matthewman
James McFetridge
Stuart Mitchell
David Monid
Tim Neal
Paul Norman
Matthew Partis
Alister Pearson
Mike Plant
Peter Rosace
Paul Thomas
J Wakeling
Chris Westbrook
Paul Williams

More books for Doctor Who fans, from www.hirstpublishing.com